Praise for
Quit Drifting, Lift the Fog, and Get Lucky

"A wonderful fable that teaches how to achieve success and how to share your wisdom with others. Implementing the lessons taught in *Quit Drifting, Lift the Fog, and Get Lucky* will help you become the person you want to be."

—Marshall Goldsmith, *New York Times* bestselling author of
What Got You Here Won't Get You There

"In *Quit Drifting, Lift the Fog, and Get Lucky* David Cottrell proves something I've been saying for years: Most successful people would not be where they are without the help of trusted advisors and mentors along the way. This little book is full of big learnings."

—Ken Blanchard, coauthor of *The New One Minute Manager*®

"This is an incredible book! The lessons are simple, profound, and doable. Implement them and you can begin achieving the success you desire."

—Lorraine Grubbs, former director of employment for
Southwest Airlines

"*Quit Drifting, Lift the Fog, and Get Lucky* is a precious gift. This book provides you with the tools and inspiration to become your very best. I encourage you to make the choice to be someone who permits others the opportunity to help you achieve success. Read this book and make that choice!"

—Larry Shaffer, senior vice president of marketing for Insperity

"*Quit Drifting, Lift the Fog, and Get Lucky* provides a fascinating perspective on how to achieve your very best, and how you can inspire others to do so as well."

—Melissa Reiff, CEO of The Container Store

"This book is loaded with great ideas to help you set your goals, overcome your obstacles and fulfill your purpose."

—Brian Tracy, author of *Maximum Achievement*

"Everyone wants the secret sauce—that one thing to help us gain faster traction toward our aspirations. *Quit Drifting, Lift the Fog, and Get Lucky* makes it clear there are many paths to follow, many ideas to consider and many people to help you along the way. I have this book handy for reflection and inspiration."

—**Valerie Sokolosky, Fox News Contributor and author of** ***Doing it Right***

"An inspiring and engaging fable about one person's journey toward success."

—**Vince Poscente,** *New York Times* **bestselling author and Olympian**

"Having a coach elevates your performance. In this engaging fable, Jack Davis is *your* personal coach. He generously shares practical wisdom and encouragement to help you realize your dreams."

—**Lee J. Colan, PhD, author of** *The Power of Positive Coaching*

"Jack Davis is probably a lot like you. Everything is fine, but something *feels* off. Through an engaging, enlightening, and gripping tale, *Quit Drifting, Lift the Fog, and Get Lucky* presents relatable and altruistic wisdom that can be easily absorbed and implemented. Enjoy this wonderful story that can steer you in a more fulfilling direction!"

—**Jordan Gross, author of** *What Happens in Tomorrow World?*

"Do not read this book. Soak it in! Pour it into every area of your life and apply the lessons. This book will move you from where you are to the person you were designed to be. Get ready to *Quit Drifting Lift the Fog, and Get Lucky*."

—**Kevin Brown, author of** *The Hero Effect*

"This book is chock full of lessons to help you become the person you want to be. The lessons taught in *Quit Drifting, Lift the Fog, and Get Lucky* are a great personal investment. It has maximum impact when shared with employees and families!"

—**Al Clark, top State Farm insurance agent 19 years in a row**

Quit Drifting,
Lift *the* Fog,
and Get Lucky

HOW TO BECOME THE PERSON YOU WANT TO BE

David Cottrell

Matt Holt Books
An Imprint of BenBella Books, Inc.
Dallas, TX

BenBella Books, Inc.
10440 N. Central Expressway
Suite 800
Dallas, TX 75231
www.benbellabooks.com
Send feedback to feedback@benbellabooks.com

BenBella is a federally registered trademark.
Matt Holt and logo are trademarks of BenBella Books.

Printed in the United States of America
10 9 8 7 6 5 4 3 2 1

Library of Congress Control Number: 2020054981
ISBN 9781953295033 (print)
ISBN 9781953295385 (ebook)

Copyediting by Scott Calamar
Proofreading by Dylan Julian
Text design and composition by
  Katie Hollister

Cover design by Paul McCarthy
Cover image © Shutterstock / pingebat (road)
  and Miroslaw Gierczyk (background)

Special discounts for bulk sales are available.
Please contact bulkorders@benbellabooks.com.

*This book is dedicated to those who
seek wisdom from mentors, exhibit the
courage to make positive changes, and
have the resolve to become the person you
want to be.*

Contents

Introduction

In the course of my career, I have studied hundreds of successful people to try to understand the secrets behind their extraordinary accomplishments. I wanted to know if there are specific guiding principles that led them to success. How do they take control of their lives? How do they maintain their energy and enthusiasm for their jobs? How do they persevere through tough times? How do they prioritize and maintain balance in their lives? Those were just a few of my questions.

I learned that success is neither accidental nor instantaneous. There are no silver bullets or scratch-and-win moves that will launch you directly to unimaginable success and happiness. And there is no grand scheme preventing you from achieving more with your life.

Success and happiness are the results of specific

actions that propel people to move forward. Also, not coincidentally, they are boosted by listening, respecting, and adhering to the guidance of trusted advisors along the way.

Unfortunately, I also found that most people do not have trusted advisors who could help lead them to become the person they want to be. They are left on their own to figure out *how* to realize their dreams. If that describes you, this book provides proven direction and encouragement that applies to you. The lessons will help you make better choices so that you can achieve the success and happiness you desire.

If you already have a mentor, this book will serve as a guide for you and your advisor to begin deeper conversations.

In *Quit Drifting, Lift the Fog, and Get Lucky*, you'll follow Jack Davis, a person like many I have known. He worked long and hard, yet his enthusiasm for work and life was running on empty. You will shadow him on his journey from struggle to charting a course that will help him achieve his very best.

If you have ever wondered, *What can I do to make things better?* the contents of the book you are holding will uncover the answer. The lessons are as trustworthy as they are simple. Don't allow their simplicity to fool you. I have seen time and time again that shortcutting any of these sessions will make your journey more challenging than it should be. They are not difficult. They are not expensive. You can do them beginning today.

Quit Drifting, Lift the Fog, and Get Lucky is written as a fable because I believe that most people can learn more by connecting with a story than from reading a lecture. In this story, you will eavesdrop on nine coaching sessions, and you'll learn, as Jack does, how to take control of your life and career.

This book can be read in one or two sittings. Read it by yourself or invite others to make the journey with you. It is easier to make changes when you have supportive people around you to encourage you, act as a sounding board, and push you to move forward. You can download a free discussion guide from www.CornerStoneLeadership.com to help you get started.

Launch your own journey toward success and make a positive difference in your life, improve relationships with those around you, and become the very best version of you.

I hope that *Quit Drifting, Lift the Fog, and Get Lucky* will help you do just that.

Meet Jack Davis

My name is Jack Davis. When I began my journey searching for success and happiness, I was probably a lot like you.

I was a good person, working hard and doing okay. I thrived during the early stages of my career, but now I felt like I was just "getting by." I'd always thought of myself as positive, confident, and driven—but lately I wondered if that was truly who I was. My self-esteem had crumbled. I was a mere shadow of who I had been in the past, and every day it seemed the happiness I wanted was slipping farther away.

The worst part was that the more I thought that way, the more it seemed to be the truth.

My frustrations at work created unrelated frustrations at home. I was happily married but my home life had become dull and routine. My health was even suffering. I wasn't making much progress, and my dreams were slowly dissolving.

I was stuck. I wanted more for myself and my family. I knew I could do better, but I needed help. I did not know where to go or what to do.

On my way home from work one day, I heard a podcaster express her views about success and happiness. One of the host's opinions was that rarely is someone "self-made." Few people, if any, had achieved significant accomplishments without the help of others. She talked about mentors who had helped guide her by sharing their experience, knowledge, passion, and wisdom. She said that without their assistance, her success probably would have never happened.

I listened, then questioned out loud: "Who are these people? Where can I find them? Is there anyone out there who would be willing to guide *me*? If I'm ever going to become the person I want to be, I need to find someone, or several people, who will help *me*."

Thus, my journey began.

This is my story. You will learn from my mentors who taught me how to take control and improve my situation.

The lessons will stimulate your thoughts, provide practical tools, and inspire you to become the person you want to be, just like they helped me.

Enjoy the journey!

JACK'S LESSONS

1.

Blast Past Tough

I began looking for mentors to share their experiences with me. I wanted to learn how they had accomplished their goals. I also wanted to know what they'd done that was different from what I was doing.

I started my search by asking my friends, neighbors, and work associates: "Who is a successful person you know who may be willing to talk to me?" Several people were suggested, but a guy named Vince Garrett was consistently mentioned. Vince was the CEO of a regional hospital network. He was one of the most respected people in town and was also known as one of the most philanthropic.

I debated: *Should I call a stranger and ask for advice?* My pride said no, but my internal voice of reason said why not? I had nothing to lose.

After I made the decision to reach out to Vince, it was a couple of weeks before I mustered the courage to actually make the call. At last, I felt the timing was right for me to take a risk and phone him.

Vince and I exchanged several messages before we connected. When I finally spoke to him, I was so nervous that I had to keep referring to the notes I'd written for myself. I briefly explained my situation and told him I was willing to do whatever was necessary to move forward to become the person I wanted to be.

Vince listened to my request and asked a few questions. After pondering for a few minutes and checking his calendar, he graciously agreed to meet with me the following Monday morning.

On Monday, I left my home for the thirty-minute drive to Vince's office. On the way, I was frustrated with myself that I had to ask for help. "This is humiliating," I muttered under my breath. "I'm just wasting my time . . . and Vince's time." Frankly, I was somewhat cynical about whether meeting with Vince would change anything. For several minutes I chastised myself and considered turning my car around to head back home. But I soon calmed down and realized that this meeting was probably necessary. I was stuck and needed help.

I arrived at Vince's office and was led to a small, private meeting room where he was completing a draft of a speech he was scheduled to deliver later that week. He immediately closed his laptop and welcomed me. Vince's voice was soft, but his tone was firm. His smile was so broad that I couldn't help but feel at ease, and his eyes were focused intently on me. My initial impression of him was that he was a kind, compassionate, and successful person.

Before taking our seats at a small, round table, Vince asked if I would like a cup of coffee. I poured my coffee into the cup and then accidently overloaded it with sugar and cream, filling it to the brim. Embarrassed and feeling foolish, I carefully drank the thick, tan mix as quickly as I could get it down.

We spent a few minutes in ice-breaking conversation and laughing about the coffee mishap. Then, Vince loosened his tie, which hung from a perfect half Windsor knot over a neatly pressed shirt, and asked, "How can I help?"

"Thanks for meeting with me," I said, then paused to clear my throat. "You were recommended by several people as someone who may be willing to share the story behind your success. I am hoping that you will provide me some words of wisdom or principles that guided you in your life and career. As I mentioned on the phone, I'm struggling pretty bad right now. I feel like I'm stuck and can't seem to find my way out on my own. I'm searching for people who I can learn from and begin moving forward again. I called you because I want to learn from you."

Vince took a sip of coffee from his mug and smiled before responding. "First, thank you for asking my opinion. I can definitely relate to your situation because I have been exactly where you are right now. It took courage for you to call. Many people will make a decision to do something to improve their situation but then fail to do anything about it. Making a decision without taking action is worthless. I'm glad my name was given to you and you made the call.

"At one time or another, everyone has to identify and address the shocking gap between what they expected from their career or life and the reality of what they are experiencing. This may be inconceivable to you now, but some things are learned best while going through a disappointing time like you are experiencing."

I nodded but it was difficult for me to believe that anything great could result from my situation. Vince continued. "Even though it's taken us a little time to get together, one thing I already admire about you is that you didn't give up on pursuing this meeting. Your perseverance and determination are great qualities. I am glad that we were able to find a time that worked for both of us."

"I know your time is valuable. Sitting down with you is important to me, and I was willing to do whatever it took to meet with you."

Vince leaned back in his chair. "I'm definitely flattered. The question you asked doesn't have an easy answer . . . principles that have meant the most to my success? Words of wisdom?" He paused before continuing. "I believe every person needs to discover their own personal keys to happiness, which involves being great at several things that are independent yet connected. Success is not a spur-of-the-moment, unrehearsed event; it is a process with ups and downs along the way.

"The situation you describe—your disappointments, struggle, and the need for help—is not unusual. One of the keys to getting back on track is to not overreact. When you're frustrated everything appears worse than it really is. It's not a good time to jump ship or make dramatic decisions. However, it's also not the time to just sit there and hope things miraculously improve, either."

"I know. That's why I'm glad I'm here."

Vince kept his eyes focused intently on me. "It's good you're seeking advice. I learned many years ago that the best way for things to improve was for me to stick my neck out a bit and seek help. Believe it or not, everyone is either in, coming out of, or headed toward a tough time—those are just a part of life. This meeting today can be your first step in making adjustments so you can become the person you want to be."

I thought for a moment, while my index finger traced the rim of my coffee cup. "It's taken me a while to get to the point of seeking advice and counsel. I'm not great at admitting I need some help."

"Not many people are," Vince said with a smile. "I wish I could wave a magic wand to improve your situation—but if I did, you might not appreciate the journey you're embarking on."

Appreciate this journey? Right, I sarcastically said to myself. But I nodded in agreement.

"It's important you accept that there is no grand conspiracy preventing you from achieving what you want in life. Success and happiness are not rigged so that some people have all the advantages and succeed, and others have all the disadvantages and fail. I doubt anyone is sitting around scheming up ways to make your life miserable. The challenges you face are not there to destroy you; they are there to redirect you to the path that's right for you.

"Instead of thinking like a victim and asking yourself,

Why is this happening to me? ask yourself, *What is this trying to teach me?* I have found that when I take a positive look at events happening *for* me instead of *to* me, I can move forward much quicker."

"That is a difficult concept to buy into," I interjected. "It is hard to find anything positive when things are falling apart. I feel that everything is happening *to* me right now. I definitely do not feel these things are happening *for* me."

Vince listened carefully before responding. "What you are feeling is a natural response. However, that may be what contributed to your situation right now. You said you were stuck. To move forward you have to accept the fact that you're not a victim. Life is full of peaks and valleys. When you fall into the victim trap, you are in a deep valley. Remaining in that trap delays your visits to the peaks."

"I hear what you are saying," I said, trying not to sound defensive. "But, doesn't everyone occasionally fall into the victim trap? I don't want to be a 'woe is me' type of person but I really don't have control over everything that has happened."

"Of course, feeling like you are a victim is natural, but focusing on those feelings will prevent you from becoming the person you want to be. It is up to you to not allow yourself to be a victim. You may not have control over everything that has happened to you, but you control your next move, which in this case was to call me. That was a good move.

"One conclusion I made while observing successful people is that they reach success and happiness when they understand and build upon their own unique talents. You can do that, too."

I chuckled self-consciously. "So how do I find out what my talents are? I don't see much to brag about. There's not a lot of good stuff going on in my life right now."

"Sure, if things were going great, we wouldn't be sitting here. If you are like most, you are probably overvaluing your weaknesses and undervaluing your talents. Many people are not mindful of where they are especially gifted. Feeling stuck and frustrated is not unusual. But *you* are unique because you're asking, questioning, searching to find out for yourself how you can become the person you want to be. Your journey will lead you to the awareness of your talents . . . you just wait and see."

Vince allowed those words to sink in before continuing. "I believe to achieve happiness and success—however you define it—you first have to feel great about yourself. Your self-esteem should not fluctuate based on your most recent or next decision. And it shouldn't be based on the economy, stock market performance, weather, or anything else that is beyond your control.

"You can't expect others to feel great about you if you don't feel great about yourself." Vince's advice was sincere and firm. "Your job performance, as well as your home life, is a reflection of your own self-image. It's difficult—almost impossible—to be great, either personally or professionally, when you don't feel great about yourself. I'm glad you came to see me, but your journey really begins with the reflection in your mirror. That may be the best advice I give you."

"I'm glad I came, too," I said, nodding. "And yes, I hear what you're saying."

"My answer to your question about the principle that has served me best is simply this: *I blast past tough.* Regardless of what happens along the way, I do whatever it takes to keep moving forward when things get tough."

"What do you mean? How do you blast through tough?"

"I found the best way to move toward a positive future is for me to take an active part in guiding it. That meant I had to accept full and total responsibility—without blaming, complaining, or making excuses. If I didn't like the results I was achieving, I first had to check my own behavior. Then, I had to quit complaining about bad luck or being in a bad situation.

"I had to take ownership of my thoughts as well as my actions"—Vince paused before continuing—"and that was difficult for me to accept. But when I looked around, blaming was not helping anything. Actually, blaming others robbed me of my power to change things. The excuses didn't improve my confidence, and my complaining was mostly to someone who couldn't do anything to fix what I was complaining about. And the grim reality was that most people didn't care about my problems. It also surprised me that many of those who *did* care were sort of glad I had them. Very seldom, if ever, did my blaming, complaining, or making excuses do any good. In fact, it was a waste of my time, emotions, and energy."

"I can relate to that," I confessed. "I'll admit I've also fallen into the blaming, complaining, and excuses district. I don't enjoy it, but it seems most people around me are also stuck there. And, quite frankly, there's not a lot going on that *is* positive, so it's easy to get caught up in the negativity."

"I understand." Vince's tone was encouraging but firm. "But I have found that very little that's worthwhile comes easy. Somewhere along the way, something or someone will get in your way, impeding your progress. Then you'll have to make a decision to retreat or blast through the tough situation.

"Never forget this: Your success and happiness will ultimately be molded by your decisions, not by temporary conditions happening around you. Closing the gap of who you are and who you want to be is dependent on what you do. Your situation may be unfair, and you may never understand why it's happening to you. Regardless, you do have a choice in how you respond—you either blast through it or yield to it. If you don't take control, your negative situation will literally consume your thoughts, actions, and enthusiasm, and as it consumes you, it will rob you of your ability to move forward."

Vince paused before continuing. "You're facing a life-changing moment right here, right now. Be thankful for it."

I squirmed uncomfortably before admitting the cold, hard facts of my situation. "Well, I assure you, I am not thankful that my life is in the stuck mode. I'm having a difficult time letting go of my anger and resentment. It's humiliating that I'm even sitting here, sharing my problems with you."

Vince wasn't alarmed at my explanation. "It may be humiliating, but you took a major step forward today when you walked through this door. Most people are surprised when *tough* pops up, but there's no reason to be surprised. *Tough* eventually shows up for everyone. It has shown up for you right here and now.

"You need to hang in there, greet the tough situation, look it squarely in the eyes, and figure out how you're going to move forward."

"So, you're saying that if I hang in there, things will improve?"

"Let me clarify that," Vince said quickly. "Unfortunately, it's not that simple. Hanging in there too long could lead to failure, as well.

"It's similar to hanging on to a rope. When you are rappelling a mountain, to make progress, you have to *hang on to* the rope with all the strength you can gather. Letting go would be catastrophic. However, suppose you are water-skiing and you lose your balance. If you continue to hang on to the ski rope, you will be thrown all over the place. In that instance, if you don't *let go* of the rope, the water will beat you to death. My point is you have to know when to hang on and when to let go."

"But how do I know when to hang on and when to let go?"

My expression prompted Vince's careful response. "That's a fair question. Your answer should contain equal doses of faith and reason. You first have to have **faith** you are pursuing the right thing for you at this juncture of your life. Then, it has to pass the ***reasonable*** test."

I noticed that Vince's voice became more serious and his gaze more penetrating. He leaned forward. "You may only want to listen to yourself . . . and you will likely only hear what you want to hear. Listen closely. Your faith needs to be verified by your trusted advisors. When you talk to them about your plan, they'll help you determine if it's reasonable. More importantly, they will make you accountable for how you will measure success."

"I have several friends who have been providing advice," I said proudly. "They want to help me. I feel pretty good about them being my advisors."

"I understand how you feel about your friends' advice but let me offer a different perspective. Speaking from my own experiences and my observations of many others, close friends do not provide great advice. They want you to pursue your dream, so they don't want to discourage you or hurt your feelings. Your advisors are critically important . . . they can make or break you. I strongly believe that the best advisors are professional acquaintances, people who have more experience than you, and who will tell you the truth from their perspective, even if it hurts your feelings. Without bias, they will confirm your faith to move forward or provide a practical reason for you to let go."

"Yeah, but . . ." I countered, "what if my situation is complicated and without an obvious answer?"

"Your advisors will help you discern whether or not your goals are realistic. If your well-thought-out answer is to stay the course, then go full speed ahead. If your answer is to let go of the dream, have the courage to make that decision. Just don't straddle the fence.

"If you decide to move forward, don't even consider quitting when you face your first obstacle." Vince emphasized, "Most of the time, people don't quit because their challenge is unreasonable or unrealistic. They give up because they get impatient. They retreat to a comfortable place, and many times they flee right before they would have found success.

"They quit because the journey is tough. Once you make the decision to move forward, you have to blast past tough even though you may be tempted to shift into neutral because you are overwhelmed. The fear of moving forward is powerful. So powerful, in fact, that it can paralyze you. Regardless of how bleak the situation appears; you have to keep moving. Don't quit. Don't panic. Saddle up. Keep moving. Begin blasting."

"That's a lot to think about."

"People who quit lose the opportunity to achieve anything significant. You have to keep moving. Spending your energy complaining, justifying, and blaming others changes nothing. It just drains away the energy you'll need to blast through your situation.

"Also, if you're like most, you'll be tempted to take shortcuts. Be careful of shortcuts. Believe it or not, most of the time the shortcuts become much longer routes."

I appreciated the wisdom Vince was sharing. "I can relate to that. I've taken shortcuts that led me back to the starting line more often than I want to admit."

Vince's assistant entered the room and announced that his next appointment had arrived.

"I'd love to continue our conversation, but I have other meetings scheduled. Let me emphasize that there is not one magical event that will catapult you to unthinkable success and happiness. Successful, happy people are not simply extraordinary people whom fate smiled on and then *boom* . . . they miraculously achieved their goals. No, they followed a plan that led them to their success and happiness. In every instance that I know of, it did not happen alone or overnight. It took years to achieve and required the help of others.

"You're off to a good start, Jack. You may have heard that saying that 'nothing changes if nothing changes.' You've made your first move. Your choices were to continue to be bitter or become better. You made your choice, now things can begin changing for the better. It's up to you to take control of your situation, right now, right where you are."

Vince stood up. "If you don't mind me asking, where are you going from here?"

"I'm not sure," I sheepishly replied. "You are the first person I have talked to, and I wasn't sure how this would work. There's something I want to clarify. Earlier you said I should be thankful for my situation. How? How can I be thankful for being stuck?"

Vince paused before answering. "You'll find out on your own. I'll bet your very best is ahead of you. And you'll realize that without blasting past the tough time you're now facing, you would never have reached your potential. Wait and see."

"I hope so," I said, but I was skeptical. "I don't feel too great about where I am right now, but I assure you I'm going to give it my best shot."

Vince seemed pleased. "Fantastic. Remember that regardless of the situation you're facing, you can make it through. I also recommend that you continue gathering information. When you do, make sure you leave with several action items from the conversation. You can use those ideas to begin building your own personal success plan."

I smiled broadly for the first time. "I will. I have several action items that surfaced in this meeting. I appreciate your encouragement and the time that you've taken to visit with me."

Then I asked a question I had been reluctant to ask earlier: "Is there someone you recommend I talk to?"

Vince thought for a few seconds. "How serious are you about making changes required for you to become the person you want to be?"

"Very serious. I am at my wits' end."

Vince looked directly at me and appeared to be assessing my sincerity. "Improving and making real progress requires discipline and following a defined process." Then, he offered more than I would have asked. "If you are willing to pay that price, I am willing to invest my time with you. The two requirements I have are that you commit to meet early every Monday morning for eight more consecutive weeks, and you commit to making changes along the way."

I was shocked. "Of course, I would be willing to learn from you. Eight weeks sounds like a long time, though. Are you sure you want to invest that amount of time with me? Is there a way we could condense it to three or four weeks?"

Vince nodded. "I hear what you are saying. However, making permanent changes requires dedicated time and participation. An eight-week time frame will give us a snapshot of almost everything that is going to get in your way and prevent you from becoming the person you want to become. It sounds like a long time, but I promise, it will go by before you know it."

"You name the time and place." I beamed, thrilled to have Vince as my mentor.

"All right. Six thirty AM beginning right here next Monday morning. We will be finished by seven thirty so you can go directly to work."

"Excellent! Thank you. You've already given me insight I could not have learned on my own or from my friends. I will see you next Monday."

I left Vince's office with mixed feelings. I was still disappointed in myself for my current situation but pleased that I called Vince for advice. And I was thrilled that Vince volunteered to mentor me and help me create my success plan.

I had taken the first step on my journey.

"BLAST PAST TOUGH" NOTES

Success and happiness will not arrive as one great, spontaneous event. It will be a combination of several interdependently connected factors.

I need mentors—people outside my normal circle of friends.

My performance reflects my self-image. I have to feel great about myself.

There is no grand conspiracy preventing me from happiness. I must take total ownership of my life without complaining, blaming, or making excuses.

Most of the time, shortcuts become the longest routes.

My challenges are not there to destroy me. They are there to redirect me to the path that is right for me.

2.

Quit Drifting

After my visit with Vince, I researched him and discovered that he was a legend in the healthcare industry. To my surprise, though, before running hospital systems, he had rescued several private and public organizations from the brink of failure and led them to success. He was considered a great visionary leader who seems to always figure out a way to keep his cool and win, even during tough times.

Monday could not arrive fast enough for me. I was eager to learn from the master.

I arrived at Vince's reception area and was escorted to

his large, well-appointed office. It was immaculate. There was no clutter on his desk or any signs of chaos that are often associated with busy people. In fact, Vince's office was the opposite; it gave the impression that everything was under control.

Vince's physical appearance reflected his calm demeanor—every hair was in its proper place, his suit looked custom made, and his polished black shoes reflected the early morning sun beaming through his window. His presence was impressive.

When I stepped into his office, I noticed a sign hanging on the wall. It had only two words: QUIT DRIFTING! *Interesting*, I thought to myself.

Vince had served on the board of directors for several organizations and was obviously ultra successful. Yet, there were no plaques, awards, or any notable signs of accomplishments around his office. The only thing hanging on his wall was the simple inscription, QUIT DRIFTING!

We exchanged pleasantries and settled comfortably into two plush, hard-back mahogany chairs. We chatted amiably for a few minutes about our favorite college football teams, and I thanked him again for taking the time to meet. I was not nearly as nervous as I was the previous Monday. He had a way of making me feel at ease.

I could not resist commenting about his pristine office

space. "I must admit that this is the most orderly work space I've ever seen. How do you keep it so organized?"

Vince grinned. "It's interesting that you noticed. It was not always like this. Early in my career, I noticed that even a little clutter would grow and eventually fill every inch of my space. It stressed me out. Several years ago, I decided to make it a priority to clean my desk before I leave every evening. I didn't realize how much my clutter affected my attitude. It may seem a little strange, but staring at a clean desk when I enter my office helps me begin my day a little better. Of course, my to-do list doesn't expand or contract based on how clean my desk is, but it helps me focus on what is important at the time."

I was fascinated. "I don't think it's strange, but it's quite different from what I am used to. I'm impressed and a little intimidated. You've already given me something to think about."

Vince then jumped into his mentoring mode. "That was a minor change that I made that helped improve my attitude. Did you have a chance to reflect on last week's meeting? Did you try anything different?"

I proceeded to share with him several actions that I took away from our previous meeting. "The most significant realization for me was the fact that I have to assume full responsibility—total ownership—without complaining, blaming, or making excuses. I have been working on changing my attitude to blasting past tough as opposed to yielding to it."

"That is a good start. However, there are many different factors that work together to help with any significant achievement. I'm not sure you can nail it down to just a couple of things. That is one reason why we will spend several weeks together talking about it. By the way, one important principle to me is written on the sign behind you. Did you see it?"

"Yes. I did," I said as I turned to look at the plaque. "When I read that message, 'Quit Drifting!' I was going to ask you what that meant."

"I'm glad you noticed. I have found that most people fall into two distinct categories—doers or drifters. The doers have purposeful intentions and are on a mission to achieve their goals. The drifters allow external circumstances to determine their next move.

"Those words—'Quit Drifting!'—remind me to stay focused on my most important priorities and to frequently check where I am in relationship to fulfilling my purpose."

That makes sense, I thought to myself. "If you don't mind me asking, what *is* your purpose?"

Vince seemed pleased to answer. "My personal objectives have evolved through the years. In my early years of marriage, my most important priority was being a great husband. When my children came along, my purpose evolved to becoming a great parent and role model as well as a great husband." Vince paused and I could see the gleam in his eyes. "Now, I have sixteen grandchildren added to the top of my importance list."

"Congratulations. That is quite a legacy you have." I could sense Vince's pride in his family.

He then showed me a photograph of him and his wife surrounded by six children, six in-laws, and sixteen grandchildren. "I know you didn't come here to listen to me talk about my family, although I love bragging about them," he said while placing the framed photo back on his credenza. "Returning to your question, in my professional life my purpose has evolved over the years as well. At my age and stage of career, my current priority is to continue to learn and improve so that I can inspire, encourage, and mentor others to help them accomplish their goals."

I was impressed by Vince's enthusiasm for life and work. "I'm glad that is the path you have chosen. If you hadn't, I may not have had an opportunity to learn from you so I can identify and pursue my own purpose."

"Absolutely. Finding and pursuing your own purpose is essential to your success and happiness. It is more than a wish or a goal; it's your purposefulness, a higher goal only you can define. It's your guide that powers everything of importance. Even though it evolves as you go through your life stages, as mine has, it has permanence and doesn't change based on temporary events that occur during each stage.

"Your purpose will help you define the image you project, how you approach life, react to surprises, and deal with things that seem unfair. I believe that my consistency of purpose and concentration on not allowing myself to drift away from it have been two important elements that have contributed to my success. One important discovery I made many years ago was that people who understand how their occupation fits into a broader reason for living are happier, more engaged, creative, and productive at work and at home."

Vince stopped and looked intently at me. "I've seen many people who have not identified a priority that they would put above everything. Then, when the next hot deal comes along, they overreact. If you're consistently creating your next new reason for being, you really don't have a compass revealing the true direction of where you are heading. You may believe you're winning, but you're not winning at all.

"Without a clear and consistent purpose, you will not be able to put a process in place to get where you want to go. You will drift. You'll move wherever the winds of the moment take you. That's not a good or productive way to exist. No one I've ever known planned to become mediocre, but most people who don't have a clearly defined purpose unintentionally allow mediocrity to seep in as they drift along.

"A friend of mine recently had an experience that illustrates what I'm talking about:

He and his wife were vacationing in Hawaii. Neither of them was a beach veteran but they decided to try snorkeling. Before going into the ocean on their own, they took snorkeling lessons in the safety of their hotel pool. Soon they were prepared for their adventure. They got their fins on and masks ready and headed toward the Pacific to discover the unseen beauty of the ocean's depths.

They were having a great time. No one else was snorkeling in the area. In fact, there was no one in sight. The water was perfect—calm, gentle, and relaxing. As they snorkeled, facedown in the water, the radiantly colored fish, spectacular plant life, and the coral reef fascinated them. It was a remarkable experience, but it was about to become unforgettable.

My friend lifted his head from the water and looked around. He quickly realized they had drifted out to sea. He could barely see their hotel in the distance. His wife was only a couple of yards from him. When he got her attention, she looked up and immediately recognized the dangerous situation they were in.

Their relaxing snorkeling adventure was over. They began swimming for their lives toward the shore. They swam for quite a while before finally reaching shallow water where they could stand up and walk to the beach. Once they reached the beach safely, they collapsed in the sand, totally exhausted.

"When they woke up that morning, they had no idea what was in store for them. They were near disaster while enjoying what they thought was a peaceful, relaxing time. They had drifted without realizing what was happening to them until they looked up. Then they were shocked to find they were not where they began and certainly not where they intended to be."

"I've heard of people drifting out to sea before, I'm glad your friends made it back to shore safely."

"Thanks, me too. Drifting is not unusual in people's personal or professional lives either. In fact, I believe most people drift occasionally. Unfortunately, rarely does anyone drift to a destination they would have chosen. They drift and then ultimately end up trying to 'swim' for their lives. They get caught up in their day-to-day activities and become distracted, disoriented, and lose perspective. Then, they look up to discover they're a long way from where they thought they'd be.

"Life doesn't have to be that way. You can choose to drift or choose to live and work with meaning and purpose. A clearly defined purpose allows you to intervene in any drift that may come your way."

I wondered out loud: "So, how do you define and live your purpose? How do you make sure you're not drifting?"

"Those are good questions." Vince's smile dissolved into cool reflection. "Since you spend the majority of your time at work, your purpose there has to be in sync with your priorities at home. It is difficult to be happy at home if your actions at work are in conflict with what you believe in. You have to be critically honest with yourself and answer some challenging questions:

"First, you have to clearly understand who you want to become. I believe that the first principle of happiness is knowing who you want to become and then having a strong desire and detailed plan to evolve into that person.

"A few good questions to ask yourself are: *How do*

I want to be described in five years? How do I want to be described in ten years? What will people say about me when they deliver my eulogy when that time comes?"

Before I had a chance to think about that, Vince suddenly changed course. "Let's take a little break here. Write in your notes your initial thoughts to these questions."

How do I want to be described in five years?

_____

_____

_____

_____

How do I want to be described in ten years?

_____

_____

_____

_____

How do I want to be remembered by the people who deliver my eulogy? _____

_____

_____

_____

_____

After allowing a few minutes for me to reflect and make notes, Vince continued. "You'll need to put more thought into this exercise, but this will help you get started. Most of the time, your initial reactions will be building blocks for you to create a more detailed plan. Once you understand who you want to become, your personal purpose will start to become crystal clear.

"After you've answered, *Who do I want to become*, ask yourself: *Am I doing the right things to develop into that person?* To prevent drifting, you have to know where you are. Look around. Which direction are you headed? Are you getting closer or further away from developing into the person you want to become?

"Another reason to look around is to recognize the powerful influence of the people you spend your time with. They are most likely reflecting the type of person you're in the process of becoming. They could be helping, or they could be hindering you from achieving your purpose. If those you spend time with are positive, hopeful, and energetic, you will probably reflect the same. But, if you spend time with people who are always making excuses about why their life is unfair, you'll tend to do the same thing. The people around you influence your actions as well as your attitude. For instance, if you spend time with people who use disrespectful language, your language will probably become like theirs. If you spend time with people with narrow viewpoints, you'll be persuaded by those views. Most of the time, people rise or sink to the level of their surroundings.

"Take a few minutes to reflect and **write the answer to** these three questions."

Based on my attitude and behaviors, who am I becoming right now?

_____

_____

_____

Who am I listening to? Are they a reflection of the person I want to become? Are they encouraging me to become my very best?

_____

_____

_____

How do people feel when they're around me? Do they feel better, the same, or worse?

_____

_____

_____

After a couple of minutes, Vince continued. "Is there a gap between who you want to become and who you are becoming?"

I wasn't pleased with my answer. In fact, I was embarrassed by some of my responses. "Yes. Even with just a short time to reflect, it's evident that there is a significant gap. I'm not very happy with where I am. I can see that I have drifted without even knowing it."

Vince was not surprised. "We all have gaps between what we want and the direction we're heading. The good news is that it's never too late to make adjustments. And most people will move over and allow anyone who knows where they are going to pass by. Now is the time for you to begin passing and closing your gap.

"Another question to answer is: *Does my work help me achieve my purpose?* Your job should be fulfilling, not a burden. It is a gift and privilege. If you come to work because it ultimately helps you accomplish your purpose, you'll enjoy it more and be more productive.

"I have seen intelligent, talented people become miserable because their purpose was out of alignment with their profession, which is where they spend most of their time. They fall into a comfortable niche and drift there instead of having a process and the discipline to pursue their purpose. They allow their careers to stall out to a predictable, boring, unfulfilling day after day at work. Every day becomes like that movie *Groundhog Day*, where you get in a cycle of doing the same things over and over."

"I get it," I had to admit. "I have been guilty of living too many 'groundhog days.' I've been going to work because it's required. It is not helping me fulfill my purpose, since my purpose has not even been defined. Maybe my unhappiness at work has created unrelated unhappiness at home. Right now, I'm not doing well in either place."

"That is probably an accurate assessment." Vince's demeanor and words were empathic, yet serious. "Your time at work should be an opportunity to help you become the person you want to be. When you intersect your personal purpose with your job requirements, work will be easier and more fulfilling. If there is a disconnect between the two, you'll likely be unhappy, unproductive, and maybe even a negative influence on those around you.

"If what you do at work does not add to your personal purpose in some way—like providing you with the funds, knowledge, skills, time, or connections with others who can help guide you toward your purpose—then you may need to make adjustments."

Vince's expression was serious. "However, it may not be necessary to change jobs to fulfill your purpose.

"For example, one person who worked with me was

happy in her job. However, she had a deep desire to spend more time with her young children. Recognizing that her children were her true purpose at that stage of her life, she changed roles at work so that she would have the flexibility to spend more time with her kids. Her new flexible hours allowed her work to add to her personal purpose at that point in her life. She sacrificed a fancier title and a few extra dollars to be able to work toward her purpose.

"Another person I knew identified his purpose as helping the less fortunate in our community. His job provided him the resources, skills, and knowledge to help hundreds of people every year. It also provided him with connections. Several of his coworkers and their friends invested their time and energy to help him fulfill his purpose. His job did not directly relate to helping the less fortunate, but it provided him the means to become the person he wanted to be. The more successful he is at his job, the more funds, knowledge, skills, time, and connections he has to help him live out his purpose and assist the less fortunate in his community.

"Long-term success and happiness require you to live within consistent operating rules that do not change based on the situation of the day. If there's one thing everyone should be able to depend upon, it's the consistency of the rules that govern you. If you know without a doubt what your purpose is, that knowledge alone will take away many of the temptations that result in mistakes."

I was intrigued. "I'm going to have to put some serious thought into this. Once I establish my purpose, should I share it with others or just keep it to myself?"

Vince then warned, "I'm glad you're proactively thinking through what you will do. You don't have to share your purpose with anyone. However, it works best when you have someone, and usually several people, who will hold you accountable. That requires they know what to hold you accountable for. Be aware, some people will not understand that your purpose drives your life instead of job titles, money, cars, or other material things that drive most people. You are more concerned about your life, not your status. That is difficult for some people to grasp.

"Another warning is that a clearly defined purpose will not suddenly make your life easy. You're still going to have the same challenges you have today. However, your outlook and response to those challenges will be different. Without a clear purpose, your tendency has probably been to overreact to an unexpected, unwanted event. When you have a clear purpose, your life will become calmer."

Vince reflected on his experience. "I learned this lesson the hard way. Early in my career, I was doing okay but I thought I could do better. The organization I was working for was going through a tough time. I became impatient. I began interviewing for a better job. I enjoyed having my ego stroked during the job interviews and began believing that I was better than my current role. Ultimately, I left a job that was providing me with a solid foundation to build my career upon in order to join an organization that offered me nothing more than a little more money. It did not take long for me to find out that I'd made a mistake. The tough time at my former organization was temporary. If I had established a clear purpose, I would not have left. I over-reacted, and that mistake set my career back several years.

"So, stay cool and calm. Don't panic. In reality, the bad is not as bad as it seems, but neither is the good as good as you think. Understanding your true purpose helps you maintain more controlled responses to whatever is happening in your life."

"You just described me," I said, jumping into the conversation. "I have been known to overreact to both the good and the bad as it happened to me. In my defense, I have to say it doesn't seem like I'm overreacting at the time it's happening, but looking back, I can see where I may have gotten a little carried away."

Vince then asked: "Have you ever heard the phrase 'This, too, shall pass'?"

"Of course. It's kind of like 'nothing lasts forever.'"

"I'm not sure where the saying originated," Vince explained, "but Abraham Lincoln shared the following story in 1859:

> It is said an Eastern monarch once charged his wise men to invent him a sentence, to be ever in view, and which should be true and appropriate in all times and situations.
>
> They presented him the words: "And this, too, shall pass away."

"Those words give us hope that, no matter what we are going through, it is temporary."

Vince suddenly stopped talking and appeared deep in thought. Then he continued, "I can attribute much of my happiness and peace to the understanding that 'this, too, shall pass.' Life is a series of emotions with great heights and great depths. The greatest highs never last forever, and the deepest lows are not permanent. Whatever is going on in your life, this, too, shall pass."

"This, too, shall pass," I repeated, even though I was not convinced that was true for me. "But I'm not sure if I will be able to pass with it. This is definitely an area that needs my attention. Is there any other advice you can give me today about purpose and drifting?"

"Since you asked . . ." Vince leaned back in his chair. "I do have a couple of bonus suggestions. First, be especially careful with your major financial decisions. I have witnessed bad money decisions destroy many people and cause them to drift into places they did not want to go. Be smart with your money. It's difficult to be great at work or at home when you are continually burdened by bad financial decisions. Do not allow debt to control your life.

"Second, you will become discouraged again somewhere along the way. You'll probably have the tendency to react to something before you get all the facts. Stay cool and don't panic. Bad things happen to even the best people. Even when a situation appears to be the worst, life is still good. Stay positive. It will help make your life better.

"My last thought to you is this: Get on with it. You probably think that you have plenty of time to begin pursuing your purpose, and you may. However, everyone is just one blood test, stress test, X-ray, or serious accident away from a life-changing moment. There's no good reason to put off becoming the person you want to be.

"Nothing would please me more than to watch you become a great role model for others to follow. People are longing to follow someone who is balanced in all areas of life. That person could be you."

"You've given me a lot to consider." I thought for a

moment and then summed up the session. "But I get what you're saying. Don't drift. Define my purpose. Create a process. Don't overreact. Control my debt. Get on with it. All of those are challenges to me. This is the straight talk I needed."

"You're on an interesting journey. My 'Quit Drifting!' philosophy is not the beginning or end of achieving success. There are many moving parts that have to work together. We will discuss more of them next week. In the meantime, complete the questions I asked you earlier. I believe your answers will be revealing to you."

I thanked Vince. As I left the office building, my mind was racing. There was a lot of new information for me to consider.

"QUIT DRIFTING" NOTES

I must clearly understand who I want to become and who I am in the process of becoming.

Drifting will not lead me where I want to go.

I need to calm down. The good is not as good as it seems; the bad is not as bad as it seems.

If I'm burdened with a persistent monthly financial crisis, I can't become the person I want to be.

I have to pay attention to those I'm hanging around. I likely will become like them, so is that helping or hurting me?

My challenges are temporary. This, too, shall pass.

3.

Hug Change

Vince seemed pleased to see me when I arrived at his office the next week. Even though I knew his schedule was jam-packed with important meetings, he made me feel that no meeting was more important than ours. I got the impression that he looked forward to sharing his knowledge and experience with me as much as I was enjoying soaking in his wisdom.

I told him about the results of the questions he'd asked last week and the changes I was making. He was pleased with my progress.

Then Vince began our session. "During this week, I

asked several of my colleagues their opinions on why they were successful. I heard some real interesting answers. Each of them was quick to acknowledge something that happened to them, but one common theme was that they had a positive role model somewhere along the way. I thought that common trait was most interesting."

"I agree with them," I chimed in. "That is the reason I called you."

"I appreciate your confidence and hope you will be able to confirm that after the next several weeks. Something I want to discuss today is a little different but has helped me throughout my career. That is, I enjoy the process of change. In fact, I believe that you should *hug change*."

"You are the first person I've ever met who said they enjoyed change. Most people I know despise and resist change."

"That's not surprising, and I believe you. I don't like change just for the sake of change, but I love the improvement that can only appear after a change has taken place. Change is as natural as breathing, yet many seem to prefer taking their last breath rather than changing. Why do you think accepting change is such a dreaded undertaking for so many?"

I thought for a few seconds. "Change is hard. Most

people are comfortable with keeping things as they are unless a crisis forces them to do things differently."

Vince nodded his agreement, then added, "That's true. Also, I think change is usually resisted because people are confined to their own perspective. In reality, everyone is limited by their experiences and personal data points. For instance, if you were raised in a military family, your perception of normal is based on the experiences you had growing up. If you were raised in a small rural town, your data points are small-town experiences. If you were raised in a large urban city, your opinions are formed by completely different data points. You also have data points based on the size of your family and your place in it, such as oldest, middle child, etc., as well as the gender of family members, religion, ethnicity, and significant personal events that molded your thinking. In most cases, your beliefs and ideas are generated from a small sample size of people whose experiences are similar to yours.

"When a change comes along, new and different data points are introduced. A natural reaction to basically anything new and different is intimidation. The unknown can be scary. You may also feel vulnerable, based on your lack of control or understanding of the new situation. When you expand your data points, your knowledge and wisdom are increased proportionally. However, even with new knowledge and wisdom, hugging change is not easy or natural. The passion and pride of your traditional viewpoint you hold on to may subconsciously overrule your ability to endorse a new perspective."

I pondered Vince's words. "So, if everyone is framed by their own data points, any change will affect everyone differently. That makes hugging change even more difficult, especially if there isn't a crisis, and some people may not see the need for any change at all."

"Exactly. A lot of people look at me as though I'm crazy when I suggest changing something that doesn't appear to be completely broken. They don't understand. I am not trying to break it; I'm trying to move forward so that we can prevent a crisis from occurring. The way I see it, if you want long-term success and happiness, adjustments are necessary and unavoidable. You have to continually make changes."

"That is unusual," I said, almost thinking out loud. "Most people would say that if it's not broken, don't fix it. In fact, I believe that as well. Why should you waste time repairing something that's not broken when there are probably plenty of other things that need fixing?"

"I've heard others make the same point many times." Vince paused, seeming to savor the moment before continuing. "That's a popular stance. I even agree that most of the time, there *are* other things that need to be fixed.

"However, regardless of what you attempt to fix, some people will be opposed to any change, even something that obviously improves their current situation. In fact, I anticipate irrational responses to any change because it will be accompanied by emotional reactions based upon people's own data points. Being a change resister instead of a change hugger is, unfortunately, human nature."

Vince rose from his chair and leaned against his desk before continuing. "A question I love to hear is: '*What would happen if?*' That simple question implies that a change will expose new possibilities. If you look at some traditional industries, you'll find many of the current leaders in those industries weren't taken seriously when they started, and in fact, they weren't even considered to be in the business in which they now excel. Uber and Lyft are transportation companies without vehicles. Airbnb is a leader in the hospitality sector and yet they don't own a room to rent. Facebook is a media leader without a newspaper or television channel. Before those organizations began, someone had to ask: '*What would happen if?*'"

I reflected on the irony of how those industry leaders thought differently from the norm and acknowledged, "Those organizations certainly disrupted their industries. I guess many companies began with someone asking: '*What would happen if?*'"

"That's right. And successful individuals ask the same question of themselves. But they add one word: '*What would happen if I* . . .'"

"I suppose you're right. Everyone has to change something to reach their next level of success. However, I think most people are like me and look to change only when they're desperate."

Vince was definitely in his element. "Your reaction is not unusual. But change should be hugged and welcomed, even when things are going well. John F. Kennedy once said, 'The time to repair the roof is when the sun is shining.' There is a lot of wisdom in that simple statement. It's foolish to wait until a storm approaches to repair the roof. However, most people won't even think about their roof until the rain is dripping on their sofa and flooding the floors. Then, they *have to* repair the roof, the sofa, and the carpet. They would rather do anything else than change . . . even if a disaster is coming.

"It's easy to become content with the status quo because it's comfortable. But you cannot improve while you are doing the same things over and over. Eventually, you have to make the decision to get out of your comfortable groove and do things differently.

"Now, I'm going to test you," Vince warned. "Have you ever heard the phrase, 'The only constant is change'?"

I thought for a moment. "I first heard it a long time ago . . . and I've heard it many times since then."

"When do you think that phrase first appeared? Was it last year . . . two years ago . . . thirty years ago . . . ?"

"Well . . ." I took a second to come up with my best guess. "I'm not sure when, but it's been around for a while. I would say Ben Franklin probably came up with it."

"Good guess, but you're about two thousand years off," Vince remarked wryly, while grinning. "Actually, Heraclitus was the first person credited with saying, 'The only constant is change,' in 500 BC, and even he probably didn't make it up. I wouldn't be surprised if he saw it on the side of a cave wall somewhere and put his name under it."

"But he could not have been envisioning the type of changes we face today," I said, turning serious.

"Probably not. Nevertheless, accepting change undoubtedly came with its own unique challenges. Then and now, everyone resists change in varying degrees. Even the smallest of changes is naturally resisted. Clearly, the message of Heraclitus two millennia ago is that change is here to stay.

"It takes a lot of courage to recognize you need to make changes. Courage is facing and dealing with anything dangerous, difficult, or painful instead of withdrawing from it. That sounds a whole lot like change, doesn't it?"

I had never connected courage with change, I acknowledged. "That's exactly what I see right now—difficulty and pain with the changes I need to make. I guess that courage and change could go hand in hand."

"They do. Change is not going away, and it takes courage to adjust to changes. So, since things will definitely change, why not hug it when it shows up? I've seen people hunker down, refuse to change, and wind up losing everything. They keep trying to *saw sawdust* at the risk of losing everything.

"There is a risk in being comfortable and unwilling to change. Comfort evolves into complacency and complacency is the root of mediocrity—success's worst enemy—even more destructive than failure. Failure can lead to success because it forces you to move in a different direction. Mediocrity, on the other hand, prevents success because it keeps you comfortable, nestled into the status quo."

Vince's tone was serious. "In order to grow, you must let go of your comfortable, traditional ways of thinking. That's the beginning of progress. Change should be embraced and hugged without fear. It allows you to move forward and look to the future with confidence."

Something about his theory was gnawing at me. "I hear

what you're saying, and I don't disagree in principle. But change is hard—sometimes really hard—for everyone."

"Change *is* hard," Vince acknowledged. "Most people prefer stability and comfort. Change typically represents the opposite—discomfort and instability—and very few people enjoy traveling into those regions."

He allowed a moment to let that sink in before continuing. "Several years ago, there was an experiment to understand reaction to change. A mouse was used to see how it responded to a minor adjustment in its environment. Here was the test:

Four tubes were placed side by side on the floor. A cube of cheese was positioned in the second tube. The mouse was released and it darted into the first tube. Finding the tube empty, the mouse scurried to the second tube. There he discovered and ate the cube of cheese, which met his basic need for survival. The mouse then returned to his home, where he had been released.

The following day, the mouse followed the same routine by dashing to the empty first tube, then moving on to the second tube where, again, he ate his cheese and returned to his home. That same routine was repeated for several days.

The mouse realized he was wasting time going to the first tube, so the next day he ran past the first tube and went directly into the second tube. There he found his cheese, ate it and returned home. That continued for several days.

Then, the researchers placed the cheese into the third tube. The following day, the mouse went directly to the second tube where his food had always been—but, alas, no cheese was in the tube.

"What do you think the mouse did? How did he react?" Vince asked.

"I suppose he went back to the first tube to look for the cheese." I guessed. "Or maybe he went to the third tube where they moved the cheese?"

"No. Checking out the third tube would have been a good choice. Instead, he chose to stay in the second tube—where his food had always been—and wait for the cheese to return to him. If allowed, the mouse would have starved in the tube as he waited for the cheese to return to where it had been.

"Doesn't that sound like the reaction of some people you know? 'Let's wait,' they say. 'We have always done it this way. It worked in the past.'"

"For sure," I had to admit—while thinking, *That mouse and I have a lot in common.*

"That experiment reinforces a couple of important lessons about hugging change. First, when a change comes along, you have to accept it, own it, and go with it . . . even though your needs may have always been met and you are comfortable with the old way. Don't sit and wait hoping that things will return to the way they were in the past. Situations are going to evolve, and improvement will not mysteriously appear without change. If you don't adjust to the change, you'll probably find yourself trying to catch up with everyone else.

"Also, when things are going well, keep looking for ways to improve. That's the best time to make positive changes. The paradox of change is the best time to do it is when it may seem to be the least necessary. You can see more clearly and experience less stress because you're not in panic mode. In the mouse experiment, a whole block of cheese could have been in the fourth tube—enough to feed his family for a year—and the mouse would not have known because he was content eating his little cube each day. The best time to adjust is when things appear to be going just fine. Remember, fix the roof while the sun is shining."

I sat in silence, trying to compose myself. I refused to completely believe what Vince was saying. "Really? What you're saying is so contrary to how most people think, it's difficult to grasp."

Vince smiled impassively. Clearly he had heard this before. "I hear you. I get it. However, there's a night-and-day difference between those who choose to take the initiative and improve and those who refuse to do things differently. I'm not talking a 10-, 20-, or even 50-percent difference. The difference in many cases is everything—success or failure, happiness or misery.

"I mentioned earlier that change requires courage because you cannot make changes without having the courage to exit from where you are comfortable. What would you say is the opposite of courage?"

After reflecting, I was confident with my answer. "I think cowardice, or maybe fear, is the opposite of courage."

"Sure, both of those answers could apply," Vince affirmed. "Some people say the opposite of courage is ignorance. Still others believe courage means not feeling fear at all. Mark Twain defined courage as 'resistance to fear, mastery of fear—but not absence of fear.' You walk forward along a path. Fear is there, too, but you keep walking.

"I think the most appropriate answer is this: The opposite of courage is conformity. Courage is having the guts and the heart to do things differently for the sake of progress. Improvement doesn't happen by taking the path of least resistance or by conforming to the way things have always been."

I found myself intrigued with Vince's perspective about change. "My resistance to change may have been one factor that contributed to the situation I'm in. That is a new realization for me."

Our allotted time was almost up. As I was preparing to leave, Vince offered another important piece of advice. "Sometimes we criticize people or our surroundings for holding us back from our dreams and aspirations. We believe that if someone else would make changes our lives would be better. However, most people underestimate the power they have to lead the change they want to happen.

"A few years ago I read a story written by an unknown monk around 1100 AD. The story goes:

When I was young, I wanted to change the world.

I found it difficult to change the world so I tried to change my nation.

I couldn't change my nation, so I tried to change my town.

I couldn't change the town and as an older man, I tried to change my family.

Now, as an old man, I realize the only thing I can change is myself. Suddenly I realized that if long ago I had changed myself, I could have made an impact on my family. My family and I could have made an impact on our town. Their impact could have changed the nation and I could indeed have changed the world.

"Don't wait to use the power you have today to change yourself and become a positive influence to those around you.

"As we wrap up this session, remember that the success of any change depends, to a large degree, upon your own attitude. You will find that when you improve your outlook about it, the alternatives on how to deal with the change will become clearer."

While Vince was leading me out of his office, he reinforced his message. "Your success and happiness will depend on you creating a personal success plan that includes everything we talk about on these Monday mornings. I believe that hugging change will be an important piece of your plan."

As I exited Vince's office, I reflected on his advice. If I am going to become the person I want to be, I have to begin unleashing my power to make the changes I need to become that person.

"HUG CHANGE" NOTES

I welcome change, even when things are going well.

I increase my data points before I make a significant change.

I must let go to grow.

All improvement requires change. Improvement will not magically appear without something changing.

The opposite of courage is conformity.

I seek to understand the perspectives of people whose ideas are the opposite of mine.

My attitude will likely determine how successful a change will be.

I have the power to improve my life today.

4.

Be Great in Small Things

W hen I arrived at Vince's office for our fourth meeting, he asked me to wait for a few minutes in the conference room. I had not been in that room before and I was amazed at the number of extraordinary awards on display. Three national publications featuring Vince accepting CEO of the Year awards were prominently showcased. *I certainly found the right person to mentor me. If anyone knows something about success, it's Vince*, I thought to myself.

Soon after, Vince entered the conference room and escorted me to his office. Along the way, he took the time to introduce me to each employee we encountered. No one seemed to be intimidated by the CEO walking around. In fact, they appeared to appreciate his presence. It was noticeable that he enjoyed a personal relationship with each of them, regardless of their role in the organization.

On the way to his office, I noticed the saying BE GREAT IN SMALL THINGS displayed in the hallway and in several cubicles. *Interesting,* I thought.

After settling into Vince's office and spending a few minutes recapping the past three sessions and the changes I was making, I asked him about the BE GREAT IN SMALL THINGS slogan that was prominently displayed throughout the offices.

"I am glad you noticed those signs. In fact, I have one here to give to you." He reached into his desk and handed me a six-by-twelve-inch framed, monogramed sign stating BE GREAT IN SMALL THINGS. "That is what we are going to talk about today. A lot of people are so absorbed in trying to accomplish big things that they neglect the small things. Those seemingly small initiatives added together consistently produce oversized and lasting results. I hope this sign will be a reminder for you."

I thanked him for the gift, and he continued, "Many

people look at our organization and assume we have something magical going on. They believe we have good fortune that can't be duplicated." He paused. "Those thoughts are absurd. Actually, any person in any organization can duplicate everything we do. It is very simple. The heart of our organization is for every person—regardless of their title or role—to 'be great in small things.' We make it our calling to provide every person we come in contact with not only what they expect from us . . . but then, a little more."

"It looks like you reinforce that principle everywhere."

"Absolutely. I give one of these signs to every employee to remind them of one of our core principles. It's a simple belief that I emphasize every day. I have found that if we are great with the small things, the big things take care of themselves. Actually, it's a life principle.

"You see, people rarely pay attention to normal. However, if you go just one small step beyond the ordinary, everyone takes notice. That's why being great in small things is so important. True greatness is reached only when you are consistently great in many little things.

"By the way, if you pay attention, you can see many familiar people and organizations delivering 'great in small things' service. It's definitely not something unique to us."

"Really?" I inquired, reluctant to believe there wasn't

something special going on in his organization. "I haven't seen any others with the number of awards you have won. I was admiring them while waiting in your conference room. Would I know any of those familiar people or organizations you label as great?"

"Of course you would." He picked up a magazine from his desk and handed it to me. "As a matter of fact, here's an article I was reading before you arrived. It is about an employee at Disney World.

"The article features someone whose job is to clean guest rooms in a Disney hotel. The story is about when she was cleaning a guest room not long ago and saw a newly purchased Mickey Mouse stuffed animal sitting in the corner. She could have just cleaned around it and left Mickey in the corner, but she chose to do a small thing. She turned on the television to the Disney channel and placed the stuffed animal on the edge of the bed. Can you imagine what those kids thought when they entered their room and saw Mickey sitting on the edge of the bed watching Disney cartoons on television? The lady whose job it was to clean the room found a way to create happiness for that family. Was that magic? Of course not, but the exhausted kids who came in the room that evening thought so. Her small act will be talked about the rest of those kids' lives."

"Disney is an excellent service organization," I thought out loud. "They do a lot of great things for their guests."

"Wait." Vince interrupted me. "You missed the point. The article is not about Disney. It is about someone who happens to work at Disney who chose to be great in small things. Disney does not teach their associates to move stuffed animals to sit in front of a television. The cleaning lady could have left Mickey sitting in the corner and she would have still done her job. But she didn't. She found a way to create happiness for the guest. And I bet she created her own happiness by that act as well. My point is that everyone can be great in the small things, regardless of whom you work for or what your role is in the organization."

"I see what you're saying. Everyone, including me, has an opportunity to be great in small things."

"I'll bet you passed some 'great in small things' organizations on your way here," Vince said modestly. "Chick-fil-A is a good example. They are flourishing in an enormously competitive business. Their success is not because of the chicken. It is about being great in several small things.

"Their 'secret sauce' is the person you come in contact with when you order. It may even be the person who comes to the drive-thru line with a menu, iPad, and smile, ready to take your order. Have you noticed, for example, that every Chick-fil-A associate has been trained to say, 'It's my pleasure' after each transaction? That's a small thing that has become a major part of their culture."

"I have noticed. But do you really think they're so successful just because they say 'It's my pleasure'? I'm not so sure about that."

Vince didn't seem surprised at my hesitation and was ready to expand his premise. "Okay. Let's think through what Chick-fil-A has to offer that is finer than their competitors. Do they have substantially better food? Do they have a more comfortable place to eat? Is their drive-thru faster? Is their restaurant the cleanest? What do you think?"

"Well . . ." I thought. "They're not really that different. Their food is good but not significantly better. The restaurants are not any more comfortable. In fact, I have to wait for a place to sit on most of my visits. The lines are long at the drive-thru. However, to their credit, they manage the drive-thru lines well and keep the lines moving. The restaurant is clean, but not noticeably cleaner than other fast-food places."

"So, why are the lines out the door?"

I thought for a few seconds. "I guess because you feel good about eating there. And the reason you feel good is probably because you are guaranteed a smile from some-one who acts like he or she cares about you."

Vince nodded in agreement and then continued. "There are plenty of chicken places. Unfortunately, it's not often that people who serve us actually tell us that it was their pleasure. In fact, in many places, the customer is treated like an unwanted necessity. Simply saying 'It's my pleasure' reflects gratitude to the people who pay for their service. The associates do not treat their customers like it's their duty, obligation, or burden to serve them. They have a desire, craving, and maybe even an obsession to treat you right.

"A simple truth is that people buy from people. When you are buying something, which type of person would you rather deal with? Someone who considers you a bur-den or someone who is obsessed about treating you right?"

"I want to do business with those who act like they like me."

"Sure you do. It may sound overly simple, but the greatest desire of everyone—whether friends, family, employees, or clients—is to be appreciated.

"Another 'great in small things' example is Ritz-Carlton, which is considered one of the best service organizations in the world. Their operating philosophy is so simple that it's brilliant. Ritz's motto is 'We are Ladies and Gentlemen serving Ladies and Gentlemen.'"

It was the first time I had heard that slogan. "That is about as simple and profound as it gets. I can see why they're so celebrated if they live that motto."

"They do. Being great in small things is among the best traits of the most impressive organizations . . . and the most remarkable people. If you do more than what is required in any field, you will stand out from everyone else. Oh, for sure you have to be positive, knowledgeable, a problem solver, and easy to do business with. But, more importantly, the most talented people are those who exhibit all of those traits, and then some.

"I have a friend, Phil Sloan, who is an example of being great in small things. Phil works at a club where I am a member. There are over four hundred members in our club, and I assure you that every one of them can provide personal examples of how Phil is great in small things. He's one of the most amazing people I've ever known. He is so great in small things that he's the gold standard. Phil takes a personal interest in me. He makes me feel terrific by asking about my family and checking up on me when I haven't shown up at the club for a few weeks He continually asks if I need anything and does everything he can to make my life easier. His consistent actions reinforce that he cares about me."

"That is pretty remarkable. What do you think has made him so great in small things?" I wanted to know.

Vince thought before responding. "I believe that some of it is because he is naturally friendly. He is also well trained, and is an avid reader. But he has a special talent greater than anyone else I know. I think Phil's main attribute is that he loves his work. He once told me: 'I love going to work because I get to meet more new people every day.' I believe he's an example of how happiness at work begins before you leave home.

"Have you noticed how most people say they 'have to' go to work?"

"Sure. Most people do have to go to work."

"Do they?" Vince questioned. "Of course you have a duty to make a living. But if you continually say you 'have to,' you sound like you're required to do something you don't want to do. I would be shocked if Phil ever woke up and told his wife, Amy, that he *had* to go to work, even though work is necessary to pay his bills. It may sound like a minor thing, but it's a negative way of looking at something important in your life. I bet as soon as Phil wakes up he tells Amy, *'I get to go to work again!'*

"I believe that to be great, you have to be like Phil

and love what you are doing. What if you changed your attitude from 'I have to go to work' to 'I get to go to work'? That one little change transforms you from being a victim who has to work into acknowledging that work is a gift and a privilege. It is a small thing, but this small thing can make a difference for you and those around you."

I contemplated what Vince had said. "I hadn't considered how my attitude toward going to work could impact my happiness or performance. That's an easy change to make. When I leave this meeting, I get to go to work again!"

Vince smiled and continued. "The 'being great in small things' philosophy can add up to major improvements for you. If you add a little something extra every day and express gratitude in every transaction, it can change your life. The fact is that most people stop when they've done the minimum required. That's when adding 'the small things' begins."

I was curious. "Is there any 'being great in small things' activity that you try to do every day?"

"That's a good question," Vince said as he pulled out a stack of personalized notes from the top drawer of his desk. "See these notes? I write at least one personal note to an employee, friend, or customer every day. It takes me about five minutes, but it's some of the most important time I spend. You'd be surprised how often people remember a short note I sent them."

"I'm not surprised. I have received complimentary emails, but I've never received a handwritten note like that out of the blue. If I were to receive one, it would be extremely meaningful."

"Complimenting people using texts or emails is good, but there is no substitution for a personal handwritten note," Vince reinforced, then added. "There are other terrific examples of actions taken by people who are great in small things. For instance, making a personal call to encourage someone has a far greater impact than leaving a voice mail or sending a text or email. Or remembering facts about friends or customers, like a birthday or significant family events, is important. Or if you make the effort to remember and call everyone by their name. Or if you volunteer for a project. You would be doing the small things that most people ignore. Those are just a few examples; there are many more small things you can do that would be meaningful.

"Don't make it complicated, because it's not. People will become loyal to you and happy to be around you if you are great in small things. You will separate yourself from those who are content to accomplish average results. They are average learners, givers, encouragers, and enthusiasts.

They are average at being average. You have far too much talent to be average. When you choose to become great in small things, you may find yourself alone—there are not that many people willing to go above average—but that's where lasting success and happiness happens.

"I am convinced that one of the chief reasons for my success has been the attitude of 'being great in small things.' It doesn't matter if you call it the extra mile, it's my pleasure, or being ladies and gentlemen serving ladies and gentlemen—what *does* matter is that you reflect what you want to reflect."

"It almost sounds too simple," I said under my breath.

"I agree," Vince said, hearing my whisper. "It's simple. Do what is expected and then some. If you are willing to do more than the minimum you are paid to do, eventually you will be paid more to do what you want to do. When you reach that point, you will be among the best. I am living proof. It may be a simple principle, but it requires that you commit to pay the price to be better than average.

"In reality, most people don't even do what they say. They might do part of it, but rarely all. It probably isn't intentional, but they just didn't follow through completely. They failed to keep their word. It is alarming how often people say a lot yet do a little. Every time they fail to live up to their word, their integrity is questioned.

"Early in my career, I learned that if I acted on what I said I would do and did my very best to do the right thing, everything else would take care of itself. Eventually you'll know what the right thing to do is, and you'll always know if what you say is true. I also learned that people forgive and forget judgment errors, but rarely does anyone forget integrity mistakes."

"I feel like my integrity has remained pretty solid even during my tough times," I responded, somewhat defensively.

"That's great. However, you may be judging it on a different scale than how the people you interact with perceive it. Many people discount simple, common, and seemingly harmless statements like 'I'll call you later,' or 'I'll keep you informed,' or 'I'll get right on it.' Then, they will forget about the commitment they made. You may believe those statements don't count, but they do. When it comes to the perspective of others, *everything* counts."

"If I'm counting those minor commitments, maybe I have slipped a little," I reluctantly admitted. "My intention is to always do what I say, but I have to confess, I will occasionally commit to some things, especially minor things, that I never get around to doing."

Vince was not surprised at my acknowledgement.

"Most people say things they don't follow through on at some time or another. Unfortunately, no one can judge whether you intended to follow through or not. They can only evaluate what you do. You may want people to allow you the grace of not counting minor commitments. But people will judge you on what *they* think about you, not what *you believe* they should think about you. My point is that everything counts when it comes to your word. Even small, minor commitments count. A friend of mine expressed it like this: 'Do what you say you're going to do. And do it a little better than you said you would.' That is a good objective for all of us."

I wasn't thrilled about what I was hearing. After thinking for a few seconds, I shared, "I've probably discounted how my integrity was being evaluated when I made what I assumed was an insignificant commitment. I believed others would judge my integrity based on major flaws like lying, stealing, embezzling, or something along those lines. Maybe I need to be more aware that everything counts, like you said."

"If someone fails to keep a small, insignificant commitment, why would you trust them with a large, significant one?" Vince asked rhetorically. "I don't think most people intentionally lie, but I've seen confidential information betrayed, resumes exaggerated. I have witnessed people take credit for someone else's work, and heard devious gossip. All of those are integrity breaches."

I admitted, "I've seen some of those same things, but I rationalized them as one of those simple little white lies everyone tells occasionally."

"Maybe everyone tells a little white lie occasionally. However, you have to ask yourself, *When is a lie small enough to not matter?* Is there a line you cross where that little lie becomes big enough to suddenly matter? If so, who determines where that line is? I don't think there is such a line. Truth is absolute, not relative. You need to be honest with 100-percent precision as best you can.

"When you think about it, it's obvious how important your word is to those around you. Everyone wants to know, without a doubt, that you will do what you say. I believe your integrity has the single greatest impact on your long-term success and happiness. It is the 'oil' that keeps relationships running smooth. It is the cornerstone of trust."

"I have not given much thought to how others judge my integrity," I admitted. "That is an area I will pay more attention to from now on."

"Your integrity is your most precious personal possession, so you have to guard and protect it." Vince spoke passionately. "Without integrity, nothing else really matters.

It doesn't matter what you say if no one trusts you. And it doesn't matter how committed, skilled, courageous, or optimistic you are if people don't believe you'll honor your words. None of those traits matter if people can't count on you to do what you say you will do. The loss of integrity is a major reason for failure and unhappiness. Look at the people who make the news every evening because of some scandal—sports figures, film stars, politicians, CEOs, or a neighbor down the street. What most of them share is that, somewhere along the way, ego and greed overrode their integrity."

"Do you have any advice on how I can guard and protect my integrity?" I was eager to know what Vince thought.

"That's another good question!" Vince was prepared to share his experience. "A person who lives with integrity is a complete person; without it you're fragmented and incomplete. So, protecting your integrity is one of the most important things you can do for your long-term happiness and success.

"I believe if you consciously do four things, you will enhance your relationships, improve trust, and become a person whom others want to be around more often.

First, ask yourself the basic integrity check: *Is the action I am about to take illegal, immoral, or unethical in any form?* If you answer yes to any of those, STOP. Period. There is never a good reason to do anything that's illegal, immoral, or unethical.

Second, ask yourself: ***What is the right thing to do?*** You will know the answer to that question. Regardless how much you may want to bury what 'right' is, if you are honest with yourself, the 'right thing' will always surface.

Third, ***defend your commitments.*** Don't make commitments you cannot keep, even the minor ones. Many people have a tough time saying no. Then they hope no one remembers they said yes to something. That is a trust-destroying habit. You may have to give up something to make your commitment. If that's the case, ask yourself: *Am I okay with making the exchange?*

Fourth, ***eliminate 'I'll try' from your commitment.*** Instead of saying 'I'll try,' tell the person either 'no' or 'consider it done.' The message you send when you say 'I'll try' is noncommittal, weak, and apathetic. You are not committed to actually doing anything when you use those words. 'Consider it done' is clear, direct, and powerful. Then, write down exactly what you committed to and make your commitment a priority.

"Of course, there are rare occasions when something

will prevent you from doing what you said. When that happens, communicate it immediately. Don't wait even a minute. People deserve time to react if you have a crisis that prevents you from doing what you said you would do. It is not fair for you to transfer your emergency to become someone else's emergency."

"That's true. I don't like assuming anyone's emergencies. However, I know I hate to make a call telling someone that I can't do what I said."

"No one enjoys making that call, but the sooner you make it, the more time and less crisis you create for someone else," Vince emphasized. "Remember, everyone wants to be around people who will live up to their word. A significant moment for me was discovering the power of the small things and the importance of absolute integrity.

"During this week, I want you to make a point of being great in small things. I think it will help make a difference in your attitude, happiness, and results. Test me on this."

"You can consider it done," I committed to Vince. "I will be more aware of how my integrity is perceived by others as well. I will report back to you next week."

As I left, it dawned on me how simple yet profound all of Vince's advice had been to me. There is plenty I can do to improve.

"BE GREAT IN SMALL THINGS" NOTES

Achieving success is not magical. It requires moving beyond the average and doing more than what was stated in my job description when I was hired.

Success begins with me feeling great about myself and others feeling great when they are around me.

Not many people travel the extra mile. I may be alone on that trip.

I have to be honest with 100-percent precision.

I have to protect and guard my integrity. It is my most precious possession.

When I make a commitment, you can confidently "consider it done."

I need to release my power and be great in small things.

5.

Lift the Fog

I left my home allowing plenty of time to spare before my meeting with Vince. I looked forward to these sessions, and I didn't want to be late. However, when I approached the bridge over the lake that I needed to cross to reach his office, it was temporarily closed to all traffic. The fog over the water was so thick I could barely see beyond the hood of my car.

I worried that Vince and I would have to postpone our meeting because of the bridge closure. I called him and explained the situation, and he immediately relieved my fear when he said, "No problem. I'll move some things around. Come after the fog lifts."

Around 8 AM the fog had lifted. The sky was clear. Almost immediately, everything changed, and I could see for miles. It was a strange shift from the dense, thick fog to a crystal clear sky.

I arrived at Vince's facility at eight fifteen. I checked in with the receptionist and waited a few minutes before Vince met me in the lobby. He greeted me with his glowing smile, self-assured handshake, and positive, energetic attitude. He confidently owned his space.

Vince led me to his office and motioned for me to sit in my usual chair across from his desk. He then began the dialogue. "Thank you for coming in this morning. I'm sorry the bridge was closed. That rarely happens. But look at the spectacular day it has become. I appreciate you calling me to let me know you would be late. I was able to move some things around; it was not a problem.

"How did it go last week?" he asked.

I was happy to share the results of improvements I had made based on our discussions. I told him I placed my BE GREAT IN SMALL THINGS sign on my desk in full view. I also told him about several changes I made to pay more attention to small things and my commitments. Then, I told him about how I sent a personal note to a friend who is going through a tough time and how that friend emailed me in response to say thanks.

Vince was pleased. "That is wonderful. You are making significant progress. Today, I want to share with you another lesson I hope you can learn from as well.

"A few years ago, I had a defining moment in my life. It occurred early in my career when I was leading another organization. We were struggling. The economy was soft, our products were behind schedule, and I was losing some of my best employees. The only things I could see at the time were a bad economy and delayed production. My personal fog was denser than the fog you faced this morning.

"That's when a friend told me that regardless of the situation I was facing, *'Something can be done, and there is always something you can do.'* Those words stuck with me, and I have leaned on them throughout my career. Without even knowing it, that person gave me a wonderful gift that changed how I looked at my personal and professional situations."

"What did you do?"

"I took him at his word. I started evaluating what was happening around me. I wrote down my thoughts about what could be done and what I could do. In that particular instance, one thing that jumped out at me was that because of the economy and production issues, I had allowed my most valuable assets—our people—to leave and go to other organizations that were facing the same issues that we were struggling with. I'll spare you all the details, but I discovered that the wisdom my friend shared with me was true. I had to adjust my focus from what was *not* happening to what *could* happen, and from *why* I could not do something to *what* I could do. It changed my perspective, and it changed my life and my career.

"Sure enough, there were things that could be done and plenty of things that I could do. Those words have been a source of hope and strength since that day. 'Something can be done'—meaning the situation is not permanent, so something can be done right now. And 'there is always something I can do'—meaning the next move is always mine to take."

"I hear what you are saying." I hesitated before continuing my thoughts. "But when I'm stuck in a situation, I have a difficult time figuring out what to do. Going forward is tricky because I can't see where I am going. It is hard for me to accept that there is *always* something that can be done. And is the next move *always* mine?"

"I understand your apprehension. But think about it." Vince then explained: "What you need to do may not be an action you can readily see. For instance, on your trip here this morning, was there anything you could do about the fog?"

"No. That was what I was thinking. There was nothing I could do to lift the fog. I was stuck." I was sure that I made my point.

"So, you called me and explained the situation. How did you feel when you called me?"

I reflected. "I was a little stressed. I worried you wouldn't be able to change our meeting time and it would be postponed or canceled. I prayed the fog would lift quickly."

"So, correct me if I'm wrong, but it appears to me you took the best course of action available to you. Lifting the fog was not something you could control, but if you'd done nothing, you would have been a no-show, and our meeting would have been canceled. You were not responsible for the foggy conditions this morning; you were responsible for the decisions you made because of the fog. You called, prayed, and had patience for the fog to lift. Something could be done . . . and you did it."

"I didn't look at calling you as taking ownership of the situation. I assumed the only appropriate action was for the fog to lift."

"I'm glad the fog rolled in this morning." Vince surprised me with his statement, and then he asked me a random question. "How much water do you think it takes to create dense fog like we had this morning?"

"I have no idea. Hundreds, maybe thousands of gallons of water?"

Vince grinned. "I read that fog covering seven city blocks, one hundred feet deep—about like our fog this morning—is composed of about one glass of water. Can you believe that small amount of water can create enough density to close a bridge? The fog was not permanent. It was a temporary state created by a very small amount of an ordinary substance.

"I believe most people create their own fog. The two great fog generators they use are constant worry and persistent negative emotions. Both worry and negative reactions create fog so thick that you can't see how to move forward."

"Yeah, but . . ." I countered, "shouldn't I worry about things that are happening in my life? I don't see how ignoring my situation would help me lift my own fog."

Vince quickly responded. "There is a difference between worry and concern. Being concerned about something can be healthy and beneficial. It is addressing a circumstance that is real. Like this morning, you were rightfully concerned about the fog. It was real; you could see it. Then, your thoughts shifted to worrying about what could possibly happen. You started worrying about things that were potentially real but were not real—changing our time, canceling the meeting, and postponing were all potential outcomes—but they were not real. You were thinking negative thoughts about things that were potentially real instead of focusing on the real facts of the situation. Real versus potentially real is the difference between concern and worry. Being concerned is okay, but worrying is destructive thinking that may eventually create unhealthy anxiety and even depression.

"Let's think about what you worry about. Earl Nightingale, one of the first personal development gurus, studied the effects of worry. He concluded that 40 percent of the time, people worry about things that will never happen. Forty percent! That's a lot of time, emotion, and energy spent on things that never happen."

I injected a little humor while displaying a wry smile. "I've heard that statistic before. It is pretty alarming when you think about it. I also heard that worrying must work since most of what we worry about never happens."

Vince laughed. "That's funny, but worrying doesn't prevent anything from happening—and that look on your face tells me you know that. The same study found that 30 percent of our worries are in the past and cannot be changed, and 12 percent are worries about criticism from others that is mostly untrue. We worry about our health 10 percent of the time, which usually only makes our health worse. Only 8 percent of our worries are real problems we'll have to face—and out of those, only half of them are under our control. Did you do the math?"

"Let's see." I referred to my notes. "Well, 40 percent never happens. Thirty percent are history. Twelve percent are probably untrue. Our health worries are 10 percent. Eight percent of what we worry about is real, but only half of those are in our control. So, maybe 4 percent are within our control. That is hard to believe."

"Yes, it is almost unbelievable. What if his numbers are off by double, triple, or quadruple? Where would we land then? How much would be within our control?"

I quickly multiplied. "We would have 8, 12, or 16 percent within our control. Those are still low numbers. According to that, worrying is a pretty bad investment of how to spend my time."

"Yes, it is." Vince agreed with my assessment. "Regardless whether the problems that you have under your control are 4 or 24 percent, that is still a small percentage of where you spend your energy worrying. Worry will paralyze you—and not much good happens when you're paralyzed by worry. That's why when someone tells you they are worried sick or worried to death, they are probably right. Worry becomes a dense fog, like we had this morning, which prevents you from seeing a path forward."

Vince then asked me, "Have you ever had the wind knocked out of you?"

"Yes. Many times during my soccer days. It's the worst feeling ever."

"It is frightening," Vince agreed and continued. "I had my wind knocked out several times in my football career. Each incident probably lasted only a few seconds, but those breathless moments seemed forever. During the time it took to recover, I could not even move.

"Worry is like having your wind knocked out. In fact, the word 'worry' comes from a word meaning 'to choke or strangle.' It is to torment oneself with disturbing thoughts. It creates fear, drains your energy, and prevents you from being your best."

"I'm guilty of worrying as much as anyone else," I acknowledged. "But I think it's human nature to worry. Is there really anything I can do to stop worrying?"

"Remember the lesson my friend taught me, something *can* be done and there is *always* something you can do," Vince reinforced. "I've put a lot of thought into why I worry and what I should be doing instead of worrying. Here are some ideas that have helped me. Write these down:

First, **stop fortune-telling**. You said you were worried this morning that I would cancel our meeting, yet I'd never given you a reason to believe that I would not be able to meet if there was an issue. Why were you worried about that? Did you think you could predict my reaction? When you don't know the true facts, the tendency is to imagine the worst—things you fear will happen—and then make assumptions based on your imagination. Those assumptions are almost always wrong. I doubt that you have a power to see the future. Quit imagining and reacting to what you don't know.

The antidote to worry is knowledge. No one is brilliant enough to make a great decision without understanding the facts. Get the facts before worrying about something that will only drain your energy. Ask yourself: *What are the real odds that what I'm worrying about will even happen?*

Next, **don't try to control the uncontrollable.** Be honest with yourself and determine what you can control. You could not prevent the fog, but you did have control over how you reacted to it. Don't allow yourself to get bogged down worrying about things that are not under your influence. Act on what you can personally control.

Then, **consider: What is the worst thing that will happen if whatever you are worrying about comes to pass?** If your worry is among the small number of things you *can* control, how will that affect your life? The worst possible outcome this morning was that our meeting would be canceled. That would probably not have been as disastrous as you thought. You could live with the eventual outcome, even though we both would have to make some changes.

Finally, **get busy, and do what you can**. If you have any control over the situation, create a plan to ensure that the worst does not happen. You will find that you don't have time to worry about things you're busy trying to improve. If you've done everything in your control, let it go. Your worrying is not helping anyone or anything. In fact, it may be making you and those around you miserable.

"It's difficult to go through that process," I admitted, genuinely wanting to understand more. "This morning's situation in the fog was different. It wasn't that complicated to call your office and let you know my situation. I don't think most solutions are that apparent."

"You may be right. Remember, though, something can be done and there is always something that you can do. When you don't know what to do, you have to create options for yourself. When I'm in that situation, I use a simple exercise that has helped me produce more potential options. Maybe this exercise will help you see more clearly when you're in the fog. Write down the numbers one through seven on a sheet of paper. Then start looking for at least seven alternatives to your situation. Don't allow yourself to stop until you find at least seven. When you think you have exhausted all the possibilities you can muster—you haven't. Find at least seven. You may have to consider possibilities that might seem 'out there.' Many times, you'll discover the best solution is the seventh one you wrote down—the one you had to dig deep and rack your brain to come up with. It could even be a combination of several different options."

After writing his suggested exercise in my notes, I looked up. "Thanks for that tip. I'm already thinking of a few situations where I can use it."

"I hope that helps," Vince continued. "Worry is one of the two great fog-creating generators. The other is negative emotions like pessimism, fear, and doubt. I have observed that successful people are positive people. Happy people are positive people. They find ways to duplicate situations when they were successful and happy, even though the current situation may be totally different. Less successful people dwell on their past failures and unhappiness and many times wind up duplicating those events.

"If you want to become your best, you have to sustain a positive, optimistic attitude. Your attitude influences your approach to life and your relationships with others. If you have a can-do attitude, you'll attract can-do people. It can be the catalyst to chart a new course for your life and help you become the person you want to be."

"Being positive during tough times is a challenge for me," I affirmed.

"It is for everyone. When you first called me, you were not real enthusiastic. You were beaten down and unable to see things to be optimistic about. And since that was noticeable to me, it was probably noticeable to everyone around you. The way you see things matters.

"I heard a story many years ago that reinforces my point:

Two researchers working for a shoe manufacturer were independently dispatched to one of the world's least developed countries. Their task was to evaluate the business potential within that country.

After several weeks, a report came back from the first researcher, and the message read, 'No market here.

Nobody wears shoes.' A few days later, the second report came back from the other researcher. It read, 'Great market here. Nobody wears shoes!'

"Those two people saw the same thing, but they saw it differently," Vince explained. "The first guy probably considered himself a realist. Like many people, he fixated on one thing and could not see the bigger picture. Actually, he was not a realist. He couldn't see the real opportunity because he was blinded by his own data points and his perception of the obstacles in front of him.

"The second guy looked beyond the obvious and saw possibilities. Optimistic people see opportunity. Negative people can't see through their own fog to the potential right in front of them."

I knew I resembled the first guy. "I can relate to that story. I probably would have been on the first plane home."

"If you had been on that plane you would not have assumed control of what was controllable. That is my point! You could have assumed control of how you looked at that situation and responded like the second guy. Your perspective was from someone who had always worn shoes. You may not consider that you could provide your knowledge and experience to make someone else's life considerably more comfortable. Your attitude could have been one of optimism, opportunity, and creating a new vision for the people around you."

"I get it." It was clear to me that the way I had looked at things in the past could have been holding me back from some of the opportunities available to me.

Vince continued sharing his experiences. "Another important lesson to remember is you get what you give."

Then, he related another story to make his point:

"Once there was a person who moved into a new town. He met a longtime resident and said, 'I'm new to your town. What are the people like here?'

'What were the people like in the town you came from?' the old-timer asked in return.

'Well, they were pretty pessimistic and always complaining, and their glasses were always half-empty, never half-full,' the newcomer replied.

'Hmmm,' said the old-timer. 'Sounds like the people who live here.'

A few weeks later, another person moved to the same town and met the same old-timer. 'I'm new to your town. What are the people like here?' the newcomer asked.

'What were the people like in the town you came from?' the old-timer asked again.

'Well, they were terrific. We worked together in the neighborhood, helped each other out, and were always there to support each other during tough times. We're going to miss them now that we've moved,' the newcomer replied.

'Hmmm,' said the old-timer. 'I think you'll like it here. That sounds like the people who live here.'"

"The old-timer's message? You get what you give. If you want to be around people who are positive, optimistic, and eager to live life, your attitude has to be the same. If you think the people around you are glum and pessimistic, check yourself, because that may be what you're reflecting, too."

I interrupted with an honest rebuttal. "I'd like to think I'm an optimistic person, but sometimes I lose my enthusiasm when the harsh reality of my situation takes over."

"Well, you're certainly not alone there," Vince agreed. "Most people respond to negative events in a negative way, which is a natural and easier response. Being optimistic in the face of a negative event takes work. The naysayers and those comfortable with negative attitudes rationalize by saying they're being 'realistic.' In most cases, that means they refuse to even acknowledge a positive response that is just as realistic.

"Do you think events in your past have created a natural negative attitude?"

"Probably," I admitted.

Vince nodded his head knowingly. "Unfortunately, we cannot change our past or the fact that people act in a certain way. Your attitude, however, is internally controlled. If you have a negative attitude, it's because you've made the choice to adopt a negative attitude. Fortunately, optimism can be learned and developed. It's a choice you can make. It's up to you."

I latched on to his comment. "How can I learn to develop optimism?"

Vince responded in his encouraging tone, "Optimism may not come naturally to you. That's okay. Give it a shot and act enthusiastic even when you may not feel like it. First you seize it, and then it has a good chance of seizing you. There are a couple of things I recommend.

"First, as we touched on in our first meeting, how you feel about yourself will greatly influence how optimistic you are about life. It begins with how you talk to yourself. If you are like most, you're far more careful and considerate with what you say to others than with what you say to yourself. Typically a large percent of self-talk is negative: 'I can't, I won't, I wish, I'm not good enough,' etc. Your best friend would never use those discouraging words about you. And you would never talk to anyone else using the same harmful words that you tell yourself.

"Even when you are stressed to the max, talk to yourself with the same manner and words you would use to encourage your best friend. When you get discouraged, ask yourself what your best friend would say to you, and then say it to yourself. It will make a difference in how you feel and in your ability to become the person you want to be.

"Second, it's good to take the time to look around. You'll see that there are plenty of things to be optimistic about, regardless of the challenges ahead. If you make it a point to list five things you're grateful for and dwell on them for a few minutes twice a day, your attitude will improve dramatically. Just five things. Taking a couple of minutes for gratitude, instead of concentrating on the things that annoy you, will help change your perspective."

"Why twice a day?" I questioned.

"I believe if you acknowledge five blessings before arriving at work, your day will naturally begin better. Regardless of what you will face, you will have a fresh perspective. In addition, before you open your door at home after work, do the same exercise. Even if you are exhausted after a tough day, refocusing on the positive things in your life will help prevent work issues from destroying your family time. The most important gift you can give your family is yourself.

Give your family your best, not just your leftovers from work."

I listened carefully. Vince's perspectives were helping me see my situation in a different light. I didn't want to leave but I realized I get to go to work today!

I told Vince, "That is some great, solid advice. You've helped me see that no one can lift my fog for me. I learned that regardless of what is going on, something can be done, and the next move is mine. Also, I know that I'm not very kind when I talk to myself. I can do better in that area as well. Thank you for sharing your time and insights with me."

"Wonderful." Vince grinned. "I have a surprise for you. During the next two weeks, I have arranged for you to meet with Alex Trevino. She has agreed to meet with you at her office at the same time we have been meeting. I think it will be good for you to hear about success and happiness from one of the finest and most influential people I know. Trust me, you will enjoy the next two Mondays."

Vince then handed me Alex's card with her office address and her personal number. "I am not sure she will be able to fill your shoes, but I have heard a lot of great things about her. I look forward to meeting her."

I left Vince and quickly wrote down some of my thoughts.

"LIFT THE FOG" NOTES

Regardless of the situation, something can be done, and there is something that I can do.

It is up to me to turn off the powerful fog machines of worry and negative emotions and lift my own fog.

I waste my time when I try to control the uncontrollable.

At least twice a day I dedicate time to focus on things I am thankful for.

I have to maintain an enthusiastic attitude if I want to attract enthusiastic people.

I look for the best in myself and eliminate negative self-talk.

I get what I give.

I give my family my best, not just the leftovers from work.

6.

Salute the Truth

I was fired up about what I had learned from Vince. I was pleasantly surprised that he, and now Alex, were willing to share their experience, passion, and wisdom with me.

I knew Alex Trevino's excellent reputation. She was the founder and CEO of a large manufacturing company that produces and ships products all over the world. Alex was legendary for her accomplishments, but I'd also heard that her route to prosperity hadn't been smooth. She had risen from being dead broke to become the mega successful person she is today. I had wanted to meet Alex for a long time but had never had the opportunity. Now, Vince had opened the door, and this was my chance.

When I arrived at her office's reception area a few minutes early for our meeting, I noticed several framed magazine covers adorning the walls. Each cover prominently featured Alex's picture. The headlines read, TURN-AROUND OF THE YEAR, RISING FROM THE ASHES, and ENTREPRENEUR OF THE YEAR. I silently nodded in admiration. Alex's accomplishments were even more inspiring than I'd heard. I couldn't help but wonder about her backstory.

At exactly our scheduled appointment time, Alex appeared. The room lit up with her energy when she entered. Her contagious smile, charisma, and impeccable attire made a splendid first impression. We walked to the conference room where she asked me about myself, my family, my time with Vince, and what I had discovered thus far. I expressed how grateful I was to meet with her. She graciously accepted my compliments.

"I'm glad Vince recommended that we get together. I enjoy sharing my experiences." Alex paused before continuing. "I don't know if you are aware, but my success did not come easy. It was preceded by devastating personal and professional failures. It was a lonely, scary time for me."

"Yes, I'm vaguely familiar with at least some of it," I said. "Your story is legendary. I had not seen the impressive magazine covers displayed in your conference room until today. That is remarkable. You've been a positive inspiration to people all over the country."

"Thanks for your kind words. It seems people enjoy reading or hearing comeback stories. Unfortunately, there is no comeback without a setback—and usually not just one, but many. I believe every successful person had to move beyond some major setbacks, which eventually helped them discover the unique road to their life accomplishments.

"I learned that lesson the hard way when my disappointments ultimately became my pathway to success. Not that long ago two major events in my life happened almost simultaneously. First, my husband Luke shocked me by informing me our marriage was on the rocks. I had no idea. I was caught completely by surprise.

"Then, shortly afterward—and again without warning—our company lost three major clients almost overnight. Suddenly, we were on the edge of bankruptcy. Our revenues had slipped a bit but I was convinced it was a temporary shortfall. It wasn't.

"I guess you could say that I was mesmerized by years of doing okay at home and at work. I was complacent. A friend once told me that there is danger in the comfort zone. That is where I found myself—I was facing danger while being content in my comfortable place—personally and professionally.

"Before those two events occurred, I was not paying attention to what was actually happening. I was seeing what I wanted to see and I blamed everyone else for my situation. In reality, my marriage had been shaky for a couple of years. At work, our products had become obsolete, our processes were antiquated, and we had new competitors who were using more efficient technology to produce products that were better than ours.

"Looking back, it was clear I made several major mistakes. I had taken my relationship with Luke for granted. At work, I hired the wrong people, rushed into decisions, didn't listen to my employees, discounted my customers' feedback, made bad financial decisions, and many other blunders. Failure, I was convinced, was not something that would happen to me.

"My personal and professional failures hit me hard. In what seemed to be the blink of an eye, my life changed forever. That is how quickly it hit me.

"My prior success had been a crummy teacher. I thought I was invincible. I found out, like everyone else, I'm vulnerable to failure. At that point I reached rock bottom, my lowest of lows. While I was deep in my own introspection, I discovered that I had ignored the harsh truth of my situation. That is when I latched onto a significant principle that changed the course of my life. It was simply that if I was going to be happy or successful, I had to learn to *salute the truth*."

I recognized Alex's humility. "Thank you for your candor. I didn't know the extent of your challenges. What do you mean when you say 'salute the truth'?"

"I learned some of my most valuable lessons through those mistakes and failures. My failures accelerated my success. They helped me discover I would not achieve my goals as long as I continued to turn my back on the truth and blame someone or something else for my botches. I was the one who took the actions, thought the thoughts, and made the choices that led me to where I was. It was me! The results of those choices were not lying.

"Walt Disney once said, 'You might not realize it when it happens, and I would not recommend it, but a kick in the teeth may be the best thing in the world for you.' Now that I've experienced a kick in my teeth and learned from it, I can agree with him.

"I learned enough from my failures to finally achieve some success again. Thanks to those experiences, I realize it's okay to fail—everyone fails at one time or another—but it's not okay to keep failing at the same thing. And it's not okay to ignore the lessons from your failures."

Alex considered my earlier question. "You asked me what it means to 'salute the truth.' I use the word 'salute' because saluting is a sign of respect and acknowledgment. In the past I would have said that I needed to welcome or embrace the truth. But I didn't want to. However, I had to respect the truth, acknowledge it, and move forward regardless of how I felt about it. One of the main reasons I failed is because I turned my back on the truth. And it's probably the same for others who fail. Not only did I not salute the truth, but I also continued to believe something was true when it wasn't."

Alex paused and reflected. "One of the toughest things to figure out is: 'What's the truth?' That sounds pretty crazy, doesn't it? Why do you think figuring out the truth is so difficult?"

I thought for a moment. "Well, maybe we don't have all the information we need to recognize the truth. Or maybe the truth changes, or it takes a long time to figure out and we arrive at the conclusion too quickly."

Alex acknowledged that each of my answers had merit in specific situations. "In addition, though, I believe some people want the truth to be different so badly, they shun reality. They either trample the truth or ignore it, just like I did.

"My truth was slippery. I tended to believe and even make up things that aligned with my hopes and dreams. And the truth was sometimes camouflaged by politics, personal agendas, pride, or feelings that blinded me. Without realizing it, I would deceive myself and believe the narrative that I desperately *wanted* to believe.

"Trust me, it's never a good idea to lie to yourself, no matter how painful the truth may be. You have to respect the truth."

I was listening intently. What she'd said had hit close to home. Although I was uncomfortable admitting my mistakes, I decided to share my experience. "I can relate to everything you just said. I guess I turned my back on the reality of my situation. There certainly wasn't any saluting going on, probably because I didn't want to admit to myself, or anyone else, that things had become as stagnant as they were. My pride would not allow me to accept the real truth. It's embarrassing. I hate that I put myself in that position."

"You're not alone," Alex said in her reassuring voice. "In my case, I was completely convinced my decisions were best for everyone—even after a decision led to failure. I was a master at confirmation bias. I would diligently seek evidence that confirmed my existing beliefs. It was easy to listen to people with opinions identical to mine. But when I did that, I avoided information that would help me see things differently and make more informed decisions.

"I confirmed my decisions with people who were similar to me—same background, values, and opinions. I asked their opinions after I had passionately expressed my own opinion to them. Actually, I was making decisions based on one opinion—mine. I had to learn to seek the perspective of those who have opinions different from mine. Looking back, it's evident why I made so many mistakes: I was not dealing with the truth.

"After coming to that realization, I decided that the real truth needed to be the catalyst for every decision in my life. I had to learn to quit making things up to look the way I wanted them to be. I was too comfortable kicking reality under the rug and trying to ignore it. That didn't do me any good."

I nodded, but inside I was squirming. The feelings she described were eerily similar to my own. "I think we all do that when we don't want to believe something."

Alex nodded in agreement, and continued. "I had to learn how to search for the truth. It was up to me to rebel against my natural tendencies to believe what I wanted to believe, and instead salute the real truth faster. I had to train myself to examine the facts and separate them from my perceptions, feelings, and ego. When I didn't understand the real truth, I corrected the wrong things.

"Once I understood what my reality was, I could make corrections and improvements. Then, my road to success became a little straighter, the challenges seemed less overwhelming, my goals were within easier reach, and I had fewer surprises along the way.

"I eventually recognized there was no need to keep learning the same thing over and over. I promised myself I would never duplicate the same mistake. Luke and I faced our marital problems head-on and made some significant changes. Thanks to Luke's courage to tell me the truth, our mutual desire to recommit to each other, and a great counselor's advice, my marriage is better than ever.

"At work, I had to make changes as well. I began hiring with greater discernment, requesting more information before making important decisions, and listening carefully to my team and our customers. My decisions became better. Then, the next time I made a mistake, I moved on without dwelling on it."

Alex paused for a moment. "I must admit that some of my failures scarred me deeply. So deep, in fact, that I became afraid to take any risks at all. My fear of failure became a powerful force against me, and I would try anything to avoid putting myself in a position where there was a chance of disappointment. I eventually came to realize that most of the really good stuff in life requires taking a risk and my fear of failure should not prevent me from trying.

"I hated failing. However, I developed strength from failure. The scars from my failures eventually healed and became beauty marks. I had to learn to not dwell on what went wrong and change my focus to what I needed to do next. When I look back, I see failure taught me humility, perseverance, and courage. I learned that my failures were important lessons that helped lead me toward my happiness and success. They also taught me to do whatever was necessary to prevent putting myself in the same situation again."

I interrupted Alex. "That's a pretty incredible realization. Your scars from your failures healed and became your beauty marks. I need to remember that."

"Yes, it *was* an incredible realization. Also, to my amazement, my greatest accomplishments arrived shortly after my most devastating defeats. After my disappointments, I had to press on and continue. To my surprise, after I was convinced that I was surrounded by insurmountable adversity, my most defining moments appeared. After that discovery, I began searching for a great triumph after every devastating disappointment . . . and you'd be surprised how often it happened.

"Your journey will have bumps along the way. Don't allow them to derail you—acknowledge the missteps, learn from them, and continue pursuing your dream. Just don't duplicate your mistakes."

I smiled half-heartedly. "I must admit, I'm surprised at your story. I made the assumption that you hadn't made the same or as many mistakes as others. But you've taught me that you had the wisdom to learn from your mistakes and make adjustments to prevent those mistakes from happening again."

"Exactly," she emphasized. "Success appears after trial, error, continued effort, and moving forward after failure. If you asked some of my friends nearing the end of their careers about their regrets, they would rarely admit to regretting things they did. Most would say they regretted *not* doing something because they had feared they might fail."

Alex paused before continuing her lesson. "Another mistake I made was believing I knew the truth before I heard the entirety of what people were saying. I was a terrible listener. I would react before the person told me everything. Unconsciously, I suppose I considered myself a psychic who could accurately read other people's thoughts like: '*This is what he really means . . . ,*' '*He thinks I don't know what he is talking about . . . ,*' '*He is going to say no . . . ,*' or '*He doesn't like me.*'"

Alex laughed at this absurdity. "Eventually, I came to accept the reality that I was not a mind reader and I couldn't know what another person was thinking until I asked them. It's a bad assumption to believe you know what anyone else is thinking. To salute the truth, you have to focus, pay close attention to what is being said, ask questions, actively listen, and acknowledge the real truth quickly."

I hesitated before I spoke. "I think everyone could probably listen better. I know I could. As you were talking, I thought you were talking about my mind-reading expertise."

"I wasn't thinking of just you, or anyone else. I was talking about me, too. I have to keep reminding myself that the biggest room in my house is the room for improvement. There's always something I can do better, more often, or with a different intensity. Becoming a better listener remains at the top of my list.

"Ironically, some of the best advice I ever received on how to improve surfaced from a friend's suggestion about how I should respond to criticism." Alex continued to share her thoughts. "I still don't like to be criticized, but criticism has helped me focus my attention on what I need to do to make better decisions."

I nodded in agreement and then admitted, "All my life, I've heard people boast, 'I welcome constructive criticism,' but I find that hard to believe. I don't like to be criticized."

"I hear you." Alex nodded. "Criticism carries a certain sting, even though it may help us correct a wrong, strengthen a weakness, or chart a better course. One reason that criticism stings is our inclination to think our idea is the best—or the only—idea that will work. If you believe that and you're closed to any suggestions, you then drown in your own stubbornness."

"So, how do you handle criticism? What did your friend suggest? I need some pointers. I either bow up and get defensive, or I shut down when someone begins criticizing me."

"I get what you are saying, Jack. I was, and sometimes I still am, defensive about criticism that comes my way. However, I've found that using criticism as a learning tool literally changed me. Here are my friend's suggestions that helped me come to that realization:

1. Recognize that **criticism is a valuable form of feedback**—and you need feedback to improve in any

area of your life. Whether the criticism is constructive or destructive, allow yourself some time to think before responding. Your emotions react faster than your thoughts, so give your thoughts time to catch up before reacting.

2. Ask yourself these questions: ***Who's offering the criticism? Are they qualified? Are they trying to hurt or trying to help? Objectively, is there any truth to what he or she is saying?***

   If the person is qualified to comment, trying to help, and there is at least a kernel of truth in what they're saying, pay close attention. They are handing you a gift . . . make sure you accept it that way.

   If the criticism is from someone who has an alternative agenda, or who is not qualified to offer constructive criticism anyway, thank them and let it go.

3. **Repeat back the criticism** as you understand it. Sometimes I would get into trouble responding to what I thought I heard, and not what was actually said. Repeating the criticism confirmed my understanding and ensured that I responded correctly.

4. Listen to what's being said but **try not to take it personally.** Don't allow your self-esteem to be at the mercy of others. The critic is not attacking you—they are criticizing your attitudes or actions.

others was actually a gift to myself. If the other person accepted my forgiveness, that was a bonus.

"Also, my forgiveness had to be a gift, not a trade exchanged with an expectation of something in return. If I expected something in return, I was not forgiving at all; I was trading. You should never include the phrase 'If I have offended you' or 'If I was wrong.' Eliminate the 'If I' and ask for their forgiveness without attachments.

"Since I will always be known by how I treat others, it was up to me to be proactive and address issues that may be lingering in the past. I could not continue to allow events in my past to consume my future."

"Your past was consuming your future?" I furiously wrote this phrase in my notes. "I can relate to that."

Alex allowed a few seconds before continuing. "Yes. Don't allow yourself to forsake your future because of your past. You have the exclusive power over your future. There is no reason for you to accept and settle for status quo or surrender as a victim of circumstances. You can take authority over your life."

Alex looked at her watch. "I have my next meeting in a few minutes, but I'll leave one last thought with you: Two common attributes I have observed among successful people are that *they do not make excuses* to justify why things are the way they are, and *they don't complain* about the way things should be. They take charge to make better things happen. They clean up the rubble from their past mistakes so that they can begin to rebuild. That is what you are doing on your visits with Vince and me. You're going to be fine."

Alex began wrapping up the session. "I enjoyed sharing my experiences. You can read about our company's comeback in those magazines you saw in our reception area. What you will not read is how my husband and I worked to get our marriage back on track. As odd as it sounds, when I look back, I can see that in due course my most difficult times became my most rewarding. I bet you will discover that, too.

"I hope this meeting was beneficial for you. Remember: Salute the truth. Regardless of how you may be tempted to manipulate it, the truth is the truth."

I was not ready to leave, but I was grateful to Alex for her time. "You are a remarkable person," I said, rising to shake her hand. "Our time together has been too short, but I'm grateful you shared your story with me. I had no idea you overcame many of the same challenges I am facing. I look forward to meeting with you again next week."

Alex continued to mentor as she escorted me toward the door. "Me, too. As you are probably discovering, success and happiness are a combination of many truths. I will share more of what I have learned next week."

I left her office feeling hopeful. The advice she'd given was both important and practical. I had been a champion at seeing what I wanted to see and believing what I wanted to believe. It was time for me to begin saluting the truth.

"SALUTE THE TRUTH" NOTES

Failure is my teacher. Pay attention. My scars from failure can become beauty marks.

I will no longer be a relentless personal self-critic.

Failure is an isolated event in my life; it is not my life.

I am not a mind reader. I need to become a great listener.

I search for a great accomplishment after a devastating disappointment. I will not allow my past to eat my future.

I ask for forgiveness for my offenses and when there is any question about my role in a situation that has become harmful.

I forgive myself, and others, without expecting anything in return.

There is no need to learn the same thing over and over. Once is enough.

7.

Ask Why

Alex had called earlier in the week to tell me she had to leave town Monday for an unexpected business trip. We agreed to meet at her residence S a t u r - day morning. While driving to my meeting with her, I reflected on everything I'd experienced in the past few weeks. I realized how fortunate I was to learn from my two mentors.

When I arrived, Alex greeted me at the front door, welcomed me into her home, and introduced me to Luke. The house was immaculate and fashionable. In her den was an endearing golden Labrador retriever, nestled close to the fire blazing in the fireplace. Then she led me into her office. It was elegant. A couple of walls were decorated with pictures of her family. Along another wall, a bookcase was packed with books, memorabilia, and photos of Alex with some of the most influential people in the state. To the left of the bookcase was a strikingly handsome vintage Italian globe on a black wooden stand. It was a warm, comfortable setting that was a pleasant place to meet. After a few minutes, we settled into soft, cozy chairs. I could tell that she enjoyed being in her relaxed surroundings.

Alex began our meeting. "I am curious. Why did you reach out to Vince?"

"When I called Vince I was at a low point in my life. I was struggling both personally and professionally and reached out to him for advice. I explained that I wanted to learn from him. I was hoping he could coach me through some changes that I needed to make to become more successful. Fortunately, he agreed and those meetings have already led me to making several personal and professional improvements."

"But, why do you want to become successful?" she asked. "Everyone wants to be successful and happy, but not many people become the very best version of themselves.

You know there's a price to be paid for success—and that price isn't cheap, either."

"Sure. If it were easy, I would already have it," I said defensively. "I want to become more successful so I can provide for my family and give back to my community. I also want to help others reach their potential. I actually want success more for what I can do with it than what it will do for me."

Alex was curious. "Jack, forgive my suspicious nature, but that sounds like a soundtrack you rehearsed before your first visit with Vince. But I'll take you at your word. So, if you find this success that you are searching for, what changes will you make in your life? To use your words, 'What are you going to do with it?'"

I reached into my notebook and pulled out a laminated sheet of paper that listed my goals. Then I shared with her a few of my professional, financial, spiritual, and physical goals. Each one included an action plan that would lead to what I was trying to accomplish.

"That is impressive. Most people don't have specific goals. Those who do generally have not written them down with a plan to achieve them. People like you who list their goals in concrete terms are far more likely to reach them. I can tell you're serious about becoming the person you want to be."

I stopped her compliment. "I must admit to you, before I began meeting with Vince, I didn't have any specific goals, much less any written down. Maybe if I had taken goal setting seriously, my call to Vince wouldn't have been necessary."

"That's even more impressive. You paid attention, and now you're making some significant changes. What process are you using for setting your goals?"

I was proud to share some of the improvements I had made. "Before a few weeks ago, I didn't have clarity on what I wanted or a process to achieve anything. When I asked myself what my goals were, my honest answer was, *I don't know.* I realized what Vince meant when he referred to drifting without purpose. My revelation was that I didn't clearly understand *what* was important to me, so how could I do the things that would get me *where* I wanted to go?"

Alex nodded. "That is a huge, important discovery. The tragedy for most people isn't that they don't achieve their goals, it's that they have not established any goals to reach. Not setting specific goals allowed you to keep your expectations low and protect yourself from disappointment. That's what may have led you to where you were—stuck. So, what did you do?"

I smiled. "Vince mentioned in one of our first sessions that I needed to listen to positive people whose advice could help me make better decisions. As I thought about what he said, one particular person came to mind who had an enormous, positive influence on my life. It was my college golf coach who I have known and respected for many years. So, I went and talked to him."

"That's a twist. What did you learn from your golf coach?"

"I had been doing a lot of reflection. I realized that when I was a student, I had specific and measurable goals. My coach was the person who introduced me to the power of setting goals. But somewhere along the way, I quit using the goal-setting process that he trained me for. So, I went to him for a refresher.

"Interestingly, my coach told me that my goals in life should follow the same process he taught me about my golf routine. Regardless of my goal, I have to see, feel, trust, and then do it if I want to achieve anything significant.

"He taught me to pursue each goal in four different ways:

First, I mentally see the goal. I visualize it as a positive situation—what I want to happen, rather than fearing what I don't want to happen. *For example, if my goal is to lose twenty pounds, I visualize myself weighing 180 pounds. I begin thinking what I look like, and how it* *feels to weigh 180. I think about the improvement it makes in my life to be at that weight.*

Second, I feel it when I write down the goal. Writing the goal on paper and describing it in positive and personal terms, and in the present tense, clarifies exactly what I want to accomplish. *I would write 'I weigh 180 on June 12.'*

Third, I trust it, so I can tell others. I share with people who will support me and hold me accountable. It's important for me to trust my decision to achieve the goal and tell others about it. Sharing my goal makes me accountable to someone other than myself and helps me move forward. And, hopefully, I can bring another person on the trip with me. *I tell them I will weigh 180 on June 12 and ask them to hold me accountable at several benchmarks along the way.*

Fourth, I do it when I take action toward the goal. I begin with a plan that includes:

- My honest assessment of my current situation. *I currently weigh 200.*
- My deadline to accomplish the goal. *On June 12, I weigh 180.*
- The anticipated obstacles I have to overcome. *I have to change my eating habits including how often*

> *I eat out, whom I eat with, and the type of foods that I eat. I also need to drink more water and less alcohol.*
- A list of the people whose help I will need. *My wife, peers, and associates need to be my encouragers.*
- My plan to accomplish the goal. *I begin tracking calories and limit myself to 2,000 calories a day. I exercise more and walk at least 10,000 steps a day.*

Finally, I make a firm decision not to tolerate anything that will get in the way of accomplishing my goal. I make a detailed list, in order of priority, that includes what I have to do to achieve my goal.

"That example is simple, but it works. It may sound crazy, but the most important thing for me was to clearly identify what I wanted. After that, I could determine what steps were needed to get it, and commit to a specific timeframe for achieving it. Then I am able to see, feel, trust, and do. It's like a recipe—if I leave out a step or an ingredient, I'm not going to get the result I want."

Alex was impressed. "That's good stuff. Why do you need to write your goals down or tell others? Why not just go to the 'do it' phase?"

"I had the same questions, but I committed to trying the full process. I discovered that when I wrote my goals on paper, it clarified my thoughts. Sometimes it's difficult for me to 'see' my goals vividly in my mind, but when I write them down, they become clear. In addition to clarifying the goal, writing it down forces me to answer two important questions: Is the goal worthwhile, and is it attainable? If the answer to either of these questions is no, I need to rethink what I am trying to accomplish.

"Then, I have to do it. It is a process that requires thought and discipline. My goals are now a part of my life. I have posted them on my mirror at home, as a screen-saver on my computers, and I have a laminated card listing my goals in my wallet. They are visible everywhere I go. I am finally realizing it's not helpful to come up with great goals and then stash them away and check back on my progress a year later. I have to follow a process and work on them every day."

"That is excellent," Alex declared. "This alone can be a game-changer for you. You're absolutely right when you say the most difficult thing is to clearly understand what you want, but it's also the most important thing. The same goal-setting process applies in all areas of your life. If you focus on improving each of those areas, you'll discover they all get stronger. I was happy to hear you talk about all four areas today. You are making real progress!"

"Vince has provided me some great suggestions,

and you taught me last week to salute the truth. That has already made a difference in my life. Is there another important attribute you believe has contributed to your success?"

"That is a good question," Alex said with a laugh. "I love questions. But before I answer, let me tell you about some of my observations. I have seen many people approach success as a zero-sum game. They believe if they are great at work, it prevents them from being great at home. They believe if they spend time on their physical health, it takes away from their spiritual health. Those are myths. They are simply not true. The successful people I know are balanced. They work hard but they do not sacrifice their family, finances, spirituality, or physical health.

"In fact, I think you can only be genuinely successful when you excel in each of those areas. They are interdependent and each of them affects your life. Your work will be better if you have a healthy body, a compassionate soul, and you feed your mind with new and positive ideas. Your home life will be better if you enjoy your work. Your work and home happiness are interwoven with each other.

"Regardless of your financial results, you will not experience success if you lose your family, health, or compassion. You have to integrate your work with the rest of your life. You don't measure success by money—you will never have the most money. Success is measured by how well you become the very best version of you."

"I agree. That's why I'm here to learn from you," I said.

"If you think about it, you might have picked up on another important principle. It's simple—*ask why.* In addition to saluting the truth, asking why was another important discovery of mine. I observed that many people cannot answer the question of *why* they are doing what they are doing. They get complacent doing the same things over and over without taking the time to ask why they're doing them or understand why it's important that they be done.

"I learned a long time ago that if I understood why things are the way they are, I could adjust to almost anything. Happiness eludes many people because they do not have a clear plan to allow it to happen. Then, when they achieve a level of success, they don't know how to handle it. You are several steps ahead of most people. You have already asked yourself *why* and are now asking others *how.*"

"Thanks. Being serious about this goal-setting process is new to me. I'm definitely a work in progress," I admitted.

"It seems to me," Alex, a connoisseur of questions, interjected, "that one of the most important questions you can ask is, 'What do you think?' That's why you are asking me and Vince about how you can improve. You've acknowledged you may not know, and others may have the answers.

To be successful, you don't need to know everything. You just need to ask the right questions and fill in the gaps of what you are missing as quickly as you can.

"I have found that, most of the time, the answers are close by. If it's a business question, your peers will probably have the answer if you ask them. If your question is about something at home, your spouse probably has the answer if you have the courage to admit you don't know and ask what they think.

"I believe your success is not very far away. It is close." Alex paused.

"Wait!" I exclaimed. "I was hoping you'd be able to provide me with a strategy. I thought that you would recommend specific actions I could take to ensure my success."

After listening carefully to me, she asked, "Do you think there is already a strategic success plan written for you? What have all of your other meetings taught you?"

I pondered for a minute and then responded. "I didn't think that a strategic plan would be written and revealed to me. But I assumed success involved more than just doing some of the basic things I've learned.

"However, reflecting on my visits with you and Vince, I think I now understand why I fell into the rut I've been in for a while. It is because I did not realize *why* it's important to blast past tough, hug change, and avoid drifting. I never considered *why* saluting the truth, protecting my integrity, or being great in small things mattered.

"It never occurred to me until you asked me *why* so many times. Now, I believe I understand *what* and *why*. None of those lessons alone will become my plan. But, if I leave even one of them out of my strategy, it will prevent me from becoming the person I want to be."

I paused and gathered my thoughts. "I guess I answered my own question. Your question of *why* is maybe the most important question I can answer about myself," I said, almost apologetically.

"I agree!" Alex confirmed my revelation. "I hope that understanding the value of asking *why* will become as important to you as it has been to me."

"I am sure it will. Your advice about saluting the truth and asking *why* is important. Thank you for spending part of your Saturday with me. I appreciate your honest reflections."

"Of course." Alex appeared pleased she was able to help me. "It was my pleasure. Remember, your past doesn't have a future, but you do. Keep learning, improving, and moving forward. The direction of your next step will reveal itself along the way."

As I left Alex's home, I was deep in thought. *I hadn't considered my journey as a puzzle before,* I said to myself.

Obviously, there is not one supernatural, perfect answer. Could all the advice that I have been given fit together for me? Without doing all of what Vince and Alex have told me, I will never be my best.

I realized with amazement that almost the entire conversation had focused on my answers to Alex's questions. It had been an enlightening experience.

"ASK WHY" NOTES

No one can create my plan for me.

Asking myself "why" helps clarify whether the price required for success is worthwhile.

Success is not a zero-sum game. Becoming my very best involves being great in each area of my life.

I don't need to know everything. I just need to fill in the gaps of what I am missing as fast as I can.

Ignoring any of the advice that Vince and Alex shared can derail my success.

8.

Get Lucky

I could hardly wait to share with Vince the lessons that Alex had taught me. I had been disappointed when he'd told me that he would not be my mentor for those two weeks, but my time with Alex was extremely valuable. Her advice was insightful and practical.

I drove to Vince's office, eager to learn more from him. When he saw me, he flashed his glowing, contagious smile. He was dressed casually but smartly in jeans and a sport coat. There was something special about Vince's smile and the way he presented himself that projected confidence and happiness.

"Greetings, Jack. I missed our meetings the past two weeks. How did it go? Did you enjoy your time with Alex? What did she say?"

"It was great. She is a terrific person. Her two lessons fit your teachings like a glove. She taught me about saluting the truth and the importance of asking why. I bet you and Alex have engaged in those discussions before."

"Ha. Strange that you caught on to that." Vince then disclosed: "Alex and I have jointly taught a success-and-happiness class at our local college for the past several semesters. The curriculum is based on our experiences, which is what we are sharing with you."

"So, I am receiving a personalized college course? I guess I got pretty lucky when I called you."

"We are both glad to help. Before we get started today, I was just reading this most interesting book." Vince held it up to show me. "It is about the positive or negative impact that Monday has on the rest of your week. According to the author, if you change your attitude about Mondays, you can change your week and change your life. It matches perfectly with what we have been discussing in our Monday morning sessions. I am going to give a copy to every member of my team. You may want to read it as well. It opened my eyes to things I once knew but forgot somewhere along the way."

He closed the book, offered me a seat nearby, and began our session. "I hope I can help a little more. When I reflect over my career, my achievements involved a combination of several significant events . . . and a little luck didn't hurt either. However, luck wasn't the driving factor. The events that helped me were created by my choices—sometimes difficult and uncomfortable choices. When all of my choices were woven together, they eventually led me to who I am today.

"Successful people struggle when making tough choices, the same as everyone else. The difference is that they are persistent. Their goals are embedded so vividly in their minds that they realize what they are trying to accomplish is worth the price of a difficult choice. Only after those choices does luck come into play. What do you think about luck?"

I didn't know where he was headed or what the right answer was, but I gave it a shot. "I think that most people have some bad luck and some good luck. The difference, I guess, is how quickly you end your bad-luck streak and how long you extend your good-luck streak."

"That's pretty accurate," Vince added. "A lot of people are confused about luck. They believe a rabbit's foot or some other lucky charm will bring forth good luck and success. They wait on good fate to fall into their lap. When that doesn't work for them, they become disappointed. They assume their unhappiness and lack of success is because of bad luck. And they mistakenly believe good luck carefully searches for a privileged few to bestow good fortunes upon.

"Luck doesn't track you down. Actually, the opposite is true . . . you must conscientiously go where luck is. You can't just want, hope, or wish for luck to show up. You must actively throw yourself in luck's path. Like you said, end your bad luck quickly and extend your good luck longer."

I interjected: "That makes sense, but where do you track down luck? There is no map that says, 'Find luck here.'"

"Of course, there aren't any luck maps. People would like for luck to show up on demand or have Siri provide the directions to take them to it. They want an instant, spontaneous combustion of luck resulting in success and happiness. The truth is, you have to meet luck where it is and ignite the fire. There is no spontaneous combustion of luck.

"Lucky people are opportunists. They are lucky because they know exactly what they need and pursue it more vigilantly than the average person. When they find it, they are prepared and pounce on their break. Unlucky people wait around for luck to show up instead of actively seeking their own luck."

Vince hesitated to make sure he had my undivided attention. "Listen very closely. This is important. Luck only appears where additional information is presented to you. You create your own luck by taking a risk and increasing your knowledge.

"Steve Jobs is one example of someone who created his own luck and pursued it vigilantly. He dropped out of Reed College after only six months. After dropping out, he hung around the school. While exploring the campus, he was intrigued that every poster and every label on each drawer on site was beautifully hand calligraphed. He decided to 'drop in' on the calligraphy class and learn about typefaces, space between different letter combinations, and other tips that make great typography.

"If he had followed the path of most dropouts in those days, he would have been a barefoot wanderer, meandering around the school, moping about how life wasn't fair. Instead, he 'dropped in' on a class that provided him information to think like an artist. His new knowledge would ultimately change the course of his life and our lives as well.

"Think about what he did. He got lucky when he learned to 'think different' by increasing his knowledge, taking a risk and seizing his opportunity.

"Other people appear to be lucky, too. However, when

you look at what made them successful, you will find that they became lucky by doing things differently. Maybe making a few more calls, working more productively, or being great in small things created their good fortune. I believe you will find—without exception—that the lucky ones pursued new information and figured out a way to seize their own opportunity.

"My philosophy about luck is very simple: *Visit where luck lives, increase your knowledge, and get lucky!* Knowledge is the power that closes the gap between your potential and your performance. The more you learn, the luckier you will be."

"That makes sense, I guess," I reasoned. "I've been out of school for quite a while, and increasing my knowledge has not been at the top of my to-do list for years. What can I do at this stage in my life to learn more and become luckier?"

Vince was swift with his response. "Most people assume their education concluded when they graduated. There is nothing further from the truth. Your most meaningful education commences after you graduate. What separates the most successful people from others is knowledge—mostly learned long after attending their last class.

"Successful people are zealous about their personal

growth. They are okay with exiting a comfortable place and allowing additional knowledge to lead them to the entrance of an unknown space that becomes their launchpad to success. You see, every time you move through an exit, you enter into a new opportunity. The only way for you to go through the entrance into the next level of your career is for you to exit your current level. That's what creating luck does—it uses the power of knowledge to exit the status quo and enter into a new beginning.

"Think about when you called me several weeks ago. What motivated you to reach out to me? Something happened to inspire you to take a risk and phone me. What was it? You never called before."

"I was listening to a podcast. The host talked about how important a mentor's advice was to her success and happiness. After listening to that program, I began searching for someone to help me. That is what led me to you."

"I am glad you were listening that day. What if you had been listening to talk radio, music, political opinions, or something else?"

"The thought to call you would not have entered my mind."

Vince asked, "So, do you think that you just got lucky that you were listening on that particular day? No. It wasn't luck. You made the choice to listen to a program where there was a possibility you could gain more information to become the person you wanted to be. You put yourself in luck's path.

"When we met and you began asking me about what contributed to my happiness and success, did your knowledge improve? Was your thinking challenged? Were you surprised at some of the answers to your questions?"

"Yes, to all of the above," I admitted.

"The reason why you're closer to success now than you've ever been before is that you have more knowledge. You uncovered the most important piece of your puzzle before you came to see me. You found out, maybe without even realizing it, that knowledge is power. The more you learn, the more valuable you become to those around you.

"Think about it. Why did you search me out? You could have chosen anyone else."

"Because someone told me that you had been where I am trying to go."

Vince stood up, put his hands on his desk, leaned forward, and looked me squarely in the eyes. Then he firmly but kindly made his point. "Exactly. People search out those who have learned the most. You visited someone who had some knowledge you were seeking. Learning from them is the fuel you need to ignite your inner fire and become the person you want to be.

"Preparing for success is not easy. It's hard work, requiring a detailed plan. You have to allocate resources and provide an accounting of your results. You also have to remain somewhat fluid to adjust to changing conditions. The most important part of your preparation for the future is to increase your knowledge today.

"You can build your own learning experiences that will help you increase your knowledge." Vince reinforced his point. "You are today what you'll be in the future, except for the people you meet and the learning experiences you create. You can be completely different or just like you are right now. Think about that. Completely different . . . or the same as you are today. So, think back. How do you compare to who you were five years ago?"

I was not excited about the answer I was about to give. "Back then, I had no idea I would be trying to figure out what success and happiness would look like five years forward. But, here I am. I haven't made much progress, if any. I didn't have a plan."

I paused before sharing a sobering thought. "I may not be as well off today as I was five years ago. That *is* embarrassing and frustrating."

Vince immediately encouraged me. "I imagine that every successful person has come to the same solemn realization that something had to change for them to become the person they wanted to be. The change made by most was to increase their knowledge faster and not allow obstacles to prevent their knowledge from expanding. Don't feel sorry for yourself. There's no time for whining. It's time for you to paint a vivid picture in your mind of who you want to be in five years and begin brushing your own canvas. You can begin making your vision a reality today."

"What do you suggest?"

"I'm glad you asked." Vince was fanatical about this subject. "The beauty of increasing your knowledge is that you don't have to leave your desk to get started. The book I was reading when you arrived is also available to you or anyone else, if you had been seeking it. Knowledge is more available today than it has ever been in history, but it still will not come looking for you . . . you have to search for it.

"Knowledge is a gift received only by persistent people, because only they will do what is needed to find it. Unlucky people never go looking for knowledge. It's up to you to go where luck is and use the information that is there. Luck resides in knowledge. Let me repeat: *Luck resides in knowledge*. One new idea has the power to transform your life forever, but you must have more knowledge to try new ideas. Don't stifle your career by limiting your knowledge.

"A lot of people say that I am lucky. I agree. However, I don't agree with most of those people on *why* I've been so fortunate. They believe luck just consistently gets in my way and I can't even avoid it. I wish that were the case. Nothing could be further from the truth.

"Luck doesn't jump into my path any more than it does anyone else's. I believe the reason I'm lucky is because I live my life by my choices, not by chance. I made a conscious decision many years ago that I would not allow my future to be determined by chance, which is unpredictable, uncontrollable, coincidental, and unplanned. I don't think that's a good way to live, and it's certainly not a good way to achieve long-term success."

I reflected on my own situation and then said, "Looking back, my choices have not been that great. Can you share with me some choices you made that helped you become lucky?"

Vince gathered his thoughts before responding. "Well, to begin with, I choose not to be a victim, regardless of how unfair I may think a situation is. I choose to commit to my goals. I choose to live my values with integrity, overcome adversity, develop positive relationships, and leave a legacy for those who will follow me. Each of those decisions is specific and important.

"If I'd just waited for luck to find me, I would never

have accumulated the knowledge I needed to become who I wanted to be. My luckiest moment was when a respected peer suggested I pursue knowledge—and then take my chances. It has worked out well for me."

"That was a wise peer and friend," I noted. "Specifically, what do you recommend I do?"

Vince was quick with his recommendation. "Invest in yourself. Most people don't make that investment, but it has a greater return than any stock or real estate venture you can buy.

"Here's my challenge to you: Read one book a month that will help you grow personally or professionally. During the next year, you'll have read twelve books. When the next job opening at a higher position comes up, would you be better prepared to assume that role because of that knowledge? Of course you would. You, too, would be lucky.

"Think of what accepting my challenge could mean to you. Most people do not read one nonfiction book in a year. Not one. However, a common trait among successful people is that they are avid readers. Many top executives read several books a month, yet their associates might not read five nonfiction books in their lifetime after completing their formal education. That's not a coincidence. Those executives understand that reading helps them see more alternatives, think more clearly, and make better decisions. In other words, it helps them become lucky!

"How long do you think it will be before you retire?" Vince's question seemed to come out of nowhere.

"Unless I get really lucky, I'll retire in fifteen years or so. It may take me a little longer, but my best guess is fifteen years."

Vince acknowledged, "You could read one hundred eighty books in fifteen years if every day you read half a chapter, which would take about ten minutes. That will make an incredible difference in your career, your life, and for those around you. And it will provide you with a much more rewarding and fulfilling retirement. I am living proof that the more you learn, the more you earn. You can, too."

I pushed back. "But I'm not a big reader. I prefer to listen to audios, watch and listen to podcasts, or watch TED Talks."

"That's fine," Vince acknowledged. "I encourage you to create your own learning experience, but you retain more knowledge when you read, underline, and touch the pages of a book than you do watching or listening to someone speak. A better suggestion is to do both. I believe that there is a direct correlation between the books you read and the success you will achieve. Read for ten minutes a day, and there's still plenty of time for any other learning experience you want to create. It's easy to agree you need to become a lifelong learner. But nothing is going to change unless you shift into creating your own luck where you are. It's a choice available to you right now.

"One more thing. Positive people attract luck like a magnet. It pulls people toward them. On the other hand, I have never known a lucky person who was negative and cynical. Never. Not once in my career have I met that person. I don't think that is an accident. If you're like me, you probably prefer to surround yourself with positive, energetic, and enthusiastic people."

I agreed. "I don't like to be around negative and cynical people, either. They tend to drag me down with them."

Vince picked up on my comment. "You're right. They will drag you down and zap your energy if you allow them. If you are not careful, you will eventually become immune to the effects negative people are having on your success and happiness. You may barely notice that you are becoming like them. It's like living next to a railroad track—after a while you don't even hear the trains. Be careful whom you choose to spend your time with."

I looked back at my notes, smiled, and said, "I had never put too much thought into evaluating whom I surrounded myself with until you told me in our second session that I would most likely become like the people I spend the most time with."

Vince was glad his point was made. "It's the truth. Most people want optimistic and enthusiastic people around them, but it takes effort. It's like the flu. If you want to catch the flu, go where people have the flu. Anytime you want to catch something, go where it already exists. Are you surrounding yourself with positive, helpful, hopeful people? If you are, you'll have a lot more reasons to remain positive, helpful, and hopeful yourself."

Vince's tone was serious. "You can tell a lot about the direction a person's life is heading by watching the people with whom they choose to spend time. More likely than not, you will become eerily similar to the people whom you hang around with. That can be a blessing or a curse. You need to be around people who bless you, not curse you. That is a decision you control."

I didn't agree completely with Vince's assessment, so I took a minute to frame my words carefully before responding. "That's good in theory, but I don't get to choose some of the people I have to be around. I deal with customers, employees, and even some family members who are not blessings to me all the time."

Vince was ready with his response. "Yes, of course everyone has to tolerate people who occasionally are not pleasant. But you can choose not to allow them to pull you down. You control your own actions.

"I believe that if you become more aware of the impact of those around you, you can make better choices. Since you will become most like those you spend your time with, who should you be spending the majority of your time with?"

"I had rather spend my time with the positive people. But, like I said, many of my relationships are beyond my control."

"I agree." Vince elaborated. "For those relationships at work, it would be great for you to encourage the negative people and lift them up. Unfortunately, it is easier for them to bring you down than for you to provide a positive push and lift them up. I encourage you to give it your best shot. At the same time, make a conscious effort to increase the amount of time you spend with the positive people. Even a 10-percent change will make a huge difference for you.

"Outside of work, you have more control. If you spend more of your discretionary time with those who lift you higher and less time with those who add stress and disorder in your life, you will naturally be happier. You can make those choices.

"To attract positive people, you must act positive. To attract successful people, you must act successful. To attract luck, you must go where additional knowledge already exists. The people whom you attract will influence the person you become. It is difficult to become a positive, committed, lucky person if you continually surround yourself with negative, lukewarm, whining people."

Vince looked at his watch. "I see we're almost out of time, but I want you to know . . . you're on a good track. Keep moving. Remember, make knowledge an intentional daily habit. The more knowledge you have, the more respect, freedom, and happiness will come your way. You will become more valuable to those around you. And, as you are aware, people seek out those who have learned the most. That is how you can become lucky, too."

I thanked Vince for his time and told him that I was looking forward to next week's lesson. He had given me great wisdom. Luck lives in knowledge. That's where I need to spend more time. I won't wait around any longer for luck to find me.

"GET LUCKY" NOTES

To get lucky, I have to go where luck is, and luck lives in knowledge.

I live my life by my choices, not by chance.

I am today what I will be in the future, except for the people I meet and the learning experiences I create.

If I want to attract positive people, I have to be positive.

The more I learn, the more I will earn.

The best investment I can make is investing in myself.

9.

Escape from Someday Isle

My lessons with Vince and Alex were nearing completion. Vince and I met at our usual time and he seemed excited to see me. "Graduation day!" he exclaimed. "You have done well. You are one of the very few people willing to invest the time, energy, and effort into correcting your path and seeking improvement. Most people wait around for things to get better and then wonder why things remain the same. Not Jack Davis! You took the initiative to proactively enrich your life."

"Thanks for your kind words. It's been interesting, revealing, and life changing," I said with a smile. "Each meeting has elevated my awareness of what I need to do to become the person I want to be. I'm eager to hear your thoughts today as well."

Vince beamed. "Actually, right now you're doing what became one of my most important beliefs about achieving success. I'm sure you were tempted to delay or even cancel your journey. You may have been afraid of where it would take you. You had to gather a great deal of courage to call and meet with someone whom you didn't know. Most people would have found a reason to wait until a more convenient time, a time that probably would have never come."

"I did put off my call to you for a while," I admitted. "Unfortunately, I only called after I had reached my wits' end."

Vince could relate to my story. "I was once exactly where you were. It took me quite a while to learn that putting things off was keeping me from getting where I wanted to go. Ironically, procrastination was my best friend. I think it's many people's closest partner. I was no different from the other people who seem to be real comfortable procrastinating.

"Then, one day I read where Calvin Coolidge stated,

'We cannot do everything at once, but *we can do something at once*!' That statement stuck with me. I *can* do something at once. That changed my perspective. There wasn't a good reason to wait around before getting started. It was a defining moment for me when I discovered that I, too, could 'do something at once.' That is what you have done by embarking on your own journey."

"I wish I'd had the wisdom to turn my back on procrastination. I think I made it my reliable companion until I couldn't go any longer. I wish—"

"Hey, you're here," Vince interrupted. "Do you see anyone else around here? Did you meet anyone else on their own journey? Did Alex or I tell you to get in line? No. There was no one waiting in line. You turned your back on procrastination when you made your first call to me.

"Rather than moving forward into an unfamiliar or uncomfortable new area, many people habitually return to Someday Isle. That's where procrastination lives, too. It's named after all the people who continually put things off. *'Someday I will,'* or *'Someday I'm going to'* are the rallying cries of the residents of Someday Isle. Never in history has a situation improved on its own while people sat basking in the sun, doing nothing on Someday Isle.

"You are not sunbathing on Someday Isle; you are

right here! You have taken positive action instead of sitting around and contemplating what your next move should be."

"I appreciate your encouragement. Do you have any specific suggestions about how I can escape Someday Isle permanently?"

Vince assembled his thoughts and then began teaching. "Absolutely. One of my core beliefs is that you own your time. It is for you to spend any way you see fit. Finding a reason to put off doing what needs to be done is always an option available to you. Don't allow yourself to take that option any longer. I know people who, unknowingly, are their most creative when they're thinking of reasons to delay something they need to do. They are too busy, too bored, too old, too young, too stressed, too comfortable—their excuses run on and on. That is not a great way to live. They will never see their possibilities or reach their potential. Happiness will only come to those whose actions rise above their excuses . . . just like you have on your journey."

I chimed in with a quick question. "So, how can I avoid the procrastination trap? Maybe I have allowed it to become a habit for me."

"That's a good question. Get ready." Vince gleamed, clearly enjoying tackling this topic. "The most basic requirement for you to escape Someday Isle is you have to assume control of your situation. One of the major sources of stress, anxiety, and unhappiness comes from feeling like your life is out of your control. You need to recognize how to take control of your time so you can take control of your life. You own your time, it is your responsibility; no one else can accept that responsibility for you."

"How can I figure out how to take control of my time and my life? A lot of things are beyond my influence."

"Sure, some things are beyond your control," Vince agreed. "However, you probably have more influence than you're giving yourself credit for. If you're like most people, you may wait around for all the stars to be aligned before you attempt to escape Someday Isle. Quit waiting around for the perfect time to get something done. Doubt, procrastination, and overanalyzing will zap your energy. You may never have as much information as you would like, but you have to seize the moment, muster your courage, and make the best decision you can. If you waited for the perfect situation, you would never get married, get promoted, have kids, or make any major decisions. There is no such thing as the perfect time. You will not get much of anything done unless you go ahead and do something before the timing is completely perfect.

"The key is that you have to 'do something at once' and take your first step off Someday Isle. Taking a first small step is far better than planning some future huge steps that are never taken.

"Also, evaluate if your task needs to be done perfectly. I've seen many people with good intentions get bogged down trying to do things perfectly, when exact precision was not worth the time or effort. Perfection paralysis is expensive. It costs you time, energy, emotions, and money. And it prevents you from accomplishing other important things. There is no good reason to spend more time than is necessary on things that simply don't require it.

"Living on Someday Isle is a frustrating habit. You have to consciously attack procrastination by having the mindset that there is no better time to get things done than right now."

"Hold on." I wanted clarification. "What about gathering all the facts so that I can make a better decision?"

Vince quickly reacted. "Procrastination begins when you delay action *after* you have the necessary information to make a decision. When you have enough facts to move forward, putting off things rarely improves your decision. In fact, realizing you have something to do that you should have already done just increases your stress.

"It may sound elementary, but to escape Someday Isle, you need to consistently create a to-do list—and then do it. The anxiety and dread you have about what needs to be done rapidly evaporates when you have a specific plan. Write down what you need to do and give yourself a deadline. If there is a task you especially dislike, do it first, and then move down your list.

"How you choose to prioritize your activities will have a huge impact on your success. A lot of people live their life in a reactionary mode that becomes like playing a neverending game of Whack-a-Mole. As soon as they knock one 'crisis' down, another pops up, and at the end of the day, they haven't accomplished anything they set out to do. One of the best questions you can ask yourself is: *If I could accomplish only one thing right now, what would that one thing be?* Your answer will quickly identify where you should direct your attention."

"Yeah," I interjected, "but what about when I'm responsible for a big assignment—one that I can't just 'do something at once' and be done with it?"

"I understand," Vince said carefully. "Sometimes a task seems too daunting to step a foot off Someday Isle and get started. If that's the case, break it down into smaller pieces and hold yourself accountable for at least getting one piece done today, another one tomorrow, etc. The hardest step you'll take is the first one. You'll be a lot happier and more productive if you 'do something at once' and have a steady stream of minor steps forward, rather than waiting for one giant leap to complete the project.

"Many people continue to live on Someday Isle because of their fear of making a decision. One way to combat that fear is to ask yourself: *How will I feel if I do nothing?* There's a cost for doing nothing, and you may find that price is not worth paying. Escaping Someday Isle requires you to be decisive.

"'Do something at once' does not mean that everything needs to be done. You may need to eliminate things that do not need to be done at all. I created a stop-doing list for myself. It contains activities that drain my time and energy without providing me much return. For instance, I had to stop checking emails constantly, stop overanalyzing, stop being outraged by opinions I read online, stop listening to gossip, some comparing myself to other people, stop keeping score when it doesn't matter, and stop saying yes when I should say no. Ask yourself, *What should be on my stop-doing list? Can I say no to some of those things and free myself up to work on more important things?* Truthfully answering those questions may be the best way to find out what actually needs to be done.

"My last tip about escaping Someday Isle is to face conflicts and bad news head-on. I have never known anyone who enjoys conflicts. However, ignoring a conflict does not cause it to go away. In fact, it nourishes it and allows it to fester and become worse. It will gnaw at and irritate you. That isn't good for anyone. Conflicts occur in all relationships. If something isn't working, face it head-on and as fast as reasonable. You are best to follow the ancient proverb and 'never leave a nail sticking up where you find it.'

"Along those same lines, when there is bad news, don't allow it to simmer until it eventually boils over. The best time to address bad news is as quickly as you can. Bad news rarely improves with age."

I couldn't resist commenting. "That's for sure. Ignoring issues and delaying bad news allows both to grow into ugly situations. I'm a witness."

Vince agreed. "I have ignored issues, too. I hoped they would just disappear, but it never happened. I had to force myself to get into the habit of saying 'do something at once, do something at once, do something at once,' three or four times a day. It became an important reminder for me to keep moving forward and get things done. That revelation has made a huge difference in my life . . . it can make a difference in your life as well."

"I understand your emphasis on 'do something at once,' but aren't there times when you need to *not* do something at once?" I questioned. "Or maybe wait before you escape Someday Isle?"

"You're one step ahead of me." Vince was pleased I was connecting with his lesson. "To be fair, there are times when it's best to wait. When you're angry is not the time to 'do something at once.' Wait, walk away, take some deep breaths, gather your emotions before you address the issue that has outraged you. When you are emotionally threatened, it is not a good time to counter with emotional threats. An angry person doesn't think clearly. It is never a good idea to call someone or send an email or text when you are angry. Sleep on it and then tackle the situation when you can do it without anger. And it would be wise to talk it through with a mentor. Having an unbiased sounding board may prevent you from saying something you'll later regret.

"Another time to wait is when you're making a major decision. Any big, life-altering decision should be made slowly and analyzed thoroughly to understand the long-term consequences. A fundamental truth is that if you can wait to make major decisions, you will have better information. All significant financial and family decisions should be done slowly."

"Doesn't your suggestion to wait contradict attacking procrastination?" I added, attempting to reconcile a few things that bothered me.

"Waiting does not contradict attacking procrastination

in those cases because procrastination does not begin until you have enough facts to move forward," Vince reminded me. "If you have all the facts available and thoroughly understand the consequences of your decision, then you can move forward without further delay.

"One main reason I've been able to achieve a level of success is because I am passionate about becoming my very best. I have found my passion in life, and work has exposed me to all kinds of possibilities. I think the same can happen to you. Achieving success and happiness is a process that requires you to 'do something at once' and escape Someday Isle, not just think about doing something."

I appreciated Vince's advice and wanted more. "Those are some great suggestions. Do you have any other time management tips that may help me?"

"I've studied time management for years—in fact it's one of my favorite pastimes—and I've discovered that there are no magic bullets when it comes to time management. I've never found anyone who had two or three hours a day they could save by doing one thing better. But, I have seen many people find an hour or two a day they could use better by doing a few things differently."

Vince had my undivided attention. My time management skills—or lack of them—had always been a challenge for me.

He continued, "Here are some simple tips that have made a difference for me.

Prioritizing is the key to time management improvement. Vilfredo Pareto, an Italian economist in the 1800s, observed that 20 percent of the people in Italy controlled 80 percent of the wealth. Then he began looking around and discovered that the 80/20 rule, now commonly known as the Pareto Principle—states that 20 percent of causes generate 80 percent of effects. It applies to many things—like 80 percent of your results will come from 20 percent of activities, 80 percent of complaints come from 20 percent of your customers, 20 percent of people consume 80 percent of your time, 20 percent of your social circle has 80 percent of its optimism—and so on. It applies to time management, as well. There are a few things you can do that will yield better results than doing a whole lot of other things. Identify and concentrate on the few priorities that yield your best return.

One of the most important activities that provides the best return for me is to set aside some uninterrupted planning time every day. Initially, it was difficult for me to discipline myself to do this, but I found that by spending twenty uninterrupted minutes planning, I could get the same amount accomplished that would take sixty minutes of normal, interrupted time. If you can't set aside twenty minutes, maybe you can set aside ten. That's still a great return for you.

Time chunk—do like activities together—so that you're not starting and stopping all the time. Batch your emails and do them at once. Return your phone calls at one time. Write memos or personal notes at one sitting. You can save a lot of time by not having to refocus on the same task several times a day. Fewer transitions from one task to another will definitely improve your productivity.

A simple tip that can give you ten, maybe fifteen minutes every day is to go to lunch earlier or later than everyone else. Why most people go to lunch at noon is a mystery to me. They wait on the elevator, wait in line at the deli, wait in line to get back on the elevator, and then complain about not having enough time for lunch. You can save half your lunch time if you go to lunch when other people don't.

Be proactive. For instance, when someone says, 'Call me later and set an appointment,' tell them, 'Let's save ourselves a call and make the appointment now.' Then it's done and you don't have to make another call just to arrange a meeting.

Beware of the time drain of social media. It is an absorber of your time, and you may not even recognize it. Social media is a convenient way to keep in touch with friends, but it is also can be a weapon of mass distraction. Decide how much of your life you are willing to allocate to social media. When you reach your time limit, turn it off. You will probably not miss anything of significance and there will be plenty of new stuff that will pop up the next day.

Finally, read a time management book. There are plenty of places where you can gain a few extra minutes every day. You may be surprised to find several tips that are important to you that may not make my list.

I interjected. "I am surprised that one common idea was missing. Is there a reason you didn't mention multitasking? That would seem to be a productive way to get more done in less time. Right?"

"Hold on, Jack. You need to be very careful determining when to multitask. If the assignment is important, you need to focus on the task at hand and not be disrupted by something that is less important. The time to multitask is when neither of the tasks are of extreme importance or require your absolute focus. If you multitask while doing multiple important things at once, you will wind up doing multiple important things badly at the same time.

Vince glanced at his watch. "Speaking of time, our time is almost up. Since this is our final session, what is your intention when you leave here?"

"My next step is to create my own specific plan using what I have learned from you and Alex. However, I don't intend on this being the last time I talk with either of you. My desire is to develop a relationship and continue to learn from both of you."

"I think that's a good strategy. We want to continue to help, too. When you first called me, you were stuck and didn't know what to do. It reminds me of another story for me to share before you leave:

Once there was a man walking down the street who fell into a hole. The hole was so deep he couldn't escape. He looked in all directions but couldn't figure out how to raise himself from the hole.

A preacher walked by, heard the man's cry for help, and inquired, 'Why are you in that hole in the road?' The man replied: 'I fell in and I can't get out.' The preacher said that he would pray for him and walked away.

A police officer walked by, heard the man's cry for help, and inquired, 'Why are you in that hole in the road?' The man replied: 'I fell in and I can't get out.' The policeman said it was against the law to be in a hole in the road, wrote him a ticket, threw it into the hole, and walked away.

An environmentalist walked by, heard the man's cry for help, and inquired, 'Why are you in that hole in the road?' The man replied, 'I fell in and I can't get out.' The environmentalist said it was environmentally unsafe to be in a hole in the road and began to picket, circling the hole and holding a sign reading, MAN IN HOLE IN ROAD . . . ENVIRONMENTALLY UNSAFE!

A friend walked by, heard the man's cry for help, and inquired, 'Why are you in that hole in the road?' The man replied, 'I fell in and I can't get out.' Without hesitation, the friend jumped into the hole with him.

The man in the hole said, 'Are you crazy? Why did you jump in this hole? I've tried the best I can, but I can't find a way out. I have a preacher praying for me, a policeman wrote me a ticket, and a goofy environmentalist picketing outside . . . and you chose to jump down here with me. Are you crazy? Why would you jump down here with me?'

The friend replied, 'Don't worry. I chose to jump in this hole with you because I've been in this hole before . . . and I know the way out!'

"You were the man in the hole," Vince explained. "Alex and I jumped in with you. Once you begin implementing your plan, it will be your turn to jump in the hole with someone else who doesn't know how to get out of his or her situation.

"Whatever you have learned is not yours to keep. It's yours to pass on to others. I'm quite certain you, too, will learn something new when you teach others. It's called 'circular learning.' That's one of the beautiful things about mentoring—the coach learns as much as, or even more than, the person who was being coached. Just as I have with you.

"Jack, I leave you with one last thing. Life is too short to not be happy, and too long to not become the very best version of you. Start having fun. Don't be so busy making a living that you forget how to live. Surround yourself with people who appreciate the unpredictable twists and turns of life. People who will lift you higher and help you maintain your sense of humor regardless of the situation. The happiest and most successful people I know have enjoyed their journey. You can, too.

"Thank you for coming to see me," Vince said as he stood up. "I know that each of the principles we discussed work. Even if you have doubts, put them to the test. This time has been valuable to me. I hope that it's been just as useful to you, and that you will permanently escape Someday Isle and begin seizing your moment."

I hated that our time was coming to a close. I enjoyed our sessions and learned more in those few weeks than I had in several years. The reality of this being our last scheduled session hit me. I tried to express one more time how grateful I was. "Your time and your insights have been incredibly valuable to me. Thank you. Each of our sessions changed my perspective and will ultimately change my life. You provided me the encouragement and direction I needed and motivated me to improve. I will never be able to repay you but I promise that I will share what I have learned with others who are trying to become the person they want to be."

As I walked to my car, I was again amazed by the simplicity of the advice I had just received. Vince and Alex were remarkable people. They had provided me advice and guidance I was eager to incorporate into my daily routine. I had been pleasantly surprised by how kindly the mentors had treated me. I learned that, as with both of them, I could be successful, confident, and likable at the same time.

My lessons were now complete. It was time for me to assimilate everything I had learned and create my personal success plan.

"ESCAPE FROM SOMEDAY ISLE" NOTES

I *"do something at once."* I will never get ahead without getting started.

I wait to respond when I am angry. I cool down and carefully consider my response.

I own my time. It is up to me to make the best use of it.

Knowing I have something to do that I should have already done increases my stress.

Perfection may not be worth its price. Perfection paralysis is expensive.

Procrastination is my enemy. I escape from Someday Isle.

Life is short. I need to start enjoying it.

From Jack Davis
to You

When I began creating my personal plan, I reflected on some of the common traits between Vince and Alex. I wrote them down: **They had an "abundance" mentality.** They were willing to share their knowledge without asking anything in return, and they weren't afraid to give away any "secrets." I learned that the biggest secret about their success was there was no secret at all. They believe there is plenty of knowledge, wisdom, and success for everyone. One person's success does not diminish the possibilities for anyone else; there is room for everyone to become their best. They were happy to help me without considering what they would receive in return.

They had each been on a unique journey of their own. They'd had challenges and weren't afraid to admit it. They were not gifted in every area of life, but they were willing to learn from other people who were better in their weak areas. They understood the power of their choices and learned to look into the future to see the consequences of the present choices they were making.

Even though they each had different talents and experiences, they were dedicated to becoming their very best. They were not just interested in becoming their best, they were committed to making it happen. They had cultivated an illustrious personal reputation by exhibiting positive action, discipline, and energy.

They worked hard. They did not work just to get paid. They were intensely focused and obsessed with making things better. It might have seemed that winning was easy for them, but winning only came after hard work.

They loved their work, and yet, they maintained balance in their lives. They learned how to integrate their careers into their lives. They believed that achieving something at all costs was not success at all and they refused to sacrifice everything in pursuit of their career. And they chose to invest their careers in something that engaged their hearts as well as their minds.

They had a healthy blend of humility and confidence.

They had a passion to study and learn from others and were quick to acknowledge the impact of other people on their lives. They were grateful and readily gave credit to those who helped them along the way. They willingly shared their wisdom with confidence. They were swift to forgive themselves and others.

The room immediately lit up when they walked in. They projected a positive image, and their appearance reflected their success. They were polished, looked their best, dressed well, and had a positive demeanor. They focused their attention on making others feel better about themselves. They asked questions and were genuinely interested in the answers. They were quick with a smile and encouragement.

Most importantly, though, **they understood the difference between existing and living.** They enjoy life because they live with purpose. They have a clear sense of direction and take positive actions daily that fulfill their purpose. They were intent on living life to the fullest while making a positive difference for those around them.

Because of my meetings with Vince and Alex, I discovered I *did*, indeed, have unique talents. My courage to ask for advice, willingness to learn, and enthusiasm for becoming the person I wanted to be were all valuable talents.

The principles shared by my mentors were a wonderful gift. I was able to begin working diligently on a defined plan to become the person I wanted to be.

I began to grasp that, no matter what happened to me, it was up to me to take responsibility and move forward into a better place. I accepted that change was essential to my improvement, and I could hug change instead of resist it. I realized I had to know, without a doubt, my purpose and not drift off course.

I became a student of my mistakes and learned to develop a "never again" response to make sure I didn't repeat them. I quit making up things I wanted to be true and began saluting the truth. I became a man of my word. When I committed to something, you could consider it done. I decided to be great in small things, and I had to consciously improve my attitude if I was to become the person I wanted to be.

I became a curious person and asked *why* more often than I had in the past. This new trait gave me the confidence to realize that what I was doing was important enough to be done well.

I learned to live in peace. I forgave those who offended me, and I forgave myself.

I read more and listened better. I was not afraid to

take action and escape Someday Isle. I got lucky when I began seeking knowledge.

My marriage got back on track. I was able to balance the important things in my life and make dedicated time for my family a priority.

I do not make the most money, live in the largest house, or drive the finest car, but I learned that my happiness was about more than those things. It was about becoming *my* very best, enjoying life, and helping others become the person they want to be.

The most important thing I learned was the joy of sharing my knowledge with everyone. This is my gift to you.

Pass it on.

From the Author

Thank you for reading this book. I hope Jack's story will become part of your own journey, as it has mine.

Throughout my life, like Jack, I have been the recipient of wonderful, fruitful advice. My desire is for you to take what you have learned in *Quit Drifting, Lift the Fog, and Get Lucky* and do two things:

1. Apply these lessons beginning today. Go back and review each chapter and develop an action plan. The key is to get started. You can get started today.

2. Don't sit on your knowledge—share it. When you lift other people up, they will lift you up. The most effective way to learn is to teach; it will clarify your ideas and reinforce your own learning. You can lead a

discussion group at work or in your community. You may want to teach those around your own dinner table as well. A free, small group discussion guide and reproducible handouts, including a time-management assessment and goal-setting process form will help you get started. You can download the free activities at www.CornerStoneLeadership.com.

What if you chose to take control of every aspect of your life? Imagine how you would feel arriving at work being thankful for your job and the people around you. How would you feel to be enthusiastic about life? How would you feel to have renewed energy so you could spend more quality time with your loved ones? How would you feel to have a marriage filled with more intimacy, joy, honesty, and friendship? How would you feel to be at peace with yourself and everyone around you?

I think you would feel magnificent. Those are choices that you can make.

As a young man, one of my heroes was professional golfer Payne Stewart, who won the US Open Championship in 1999. Shortly after that victory, he perished in a tragic airplane accident. Payne was a charismatic, fun-loving guy who had a passion for his work, combined with a deep faith in his purpose. Shortly before his death, he was quoted as saying: "The thing about dreams is sometimes you get to live them out."

That is how I feel about my career. I am living out my dreams. One of my dreams is to encourage you to become your best in whatever dream you have chosen for your life.

I urge you to open your eyes . . . wide open. Go share with your family how much they mean to you. Go tell the people at work how thankful you are for your job. Enjoy the grace of today. Passionately pursue your true purpose with no remorse, no regrets, all-in, all the time.

If you do, you will discover with astonishment, amazement, and humbleness—as I did—that life's greatest rewards appear in some of the most unexpected places. They are ready to be discovered.

My hope is that *Quit Drifting, Lift the Fog, and Get Lucky* will provide you with encouragement and knowledge so you will make the decision to become the person you want to be. You can and you should become that person.

The next move is always yours. This is your life, your time, and your opportunity.

May life's journey bring you happiness and success.

—David Cottrell
Boerne, Texas

Acknowledgments

I have been one of the most fortunate people in the world because of my faith, family, friends, and associates. I have been molded and formed by those whom I have been fortunate enough to have on my team.

Thanks to my friends who have encouraged me and have taken the time to make me a part of their lives. I am especially grateful to Louis Kruger, Mark Layton, Tod Taylor, Bryan Lancaster, Bob Biddle, Arlen Espinal, and Paul Liberato.

Thanks to the CornerStone team: Barbara Bartlett, Ken Carnes, Lee Colan, Melissa Farr, Harry Hopkins, Michele Lucia, and our customers who have remained loyal to CornerStone for the past twenty-five years. The contents in this book reflect many of the lessons I learned from you. Please accept my deepest gratitude.

Special credits to Matt Holt and his fabulous team. In my book, Matt is the shining star in the publishing world. Sincere appreciation to editor Claire Schulz, copy editor Scott Calamar, production editor Katie Hollister, and marketer Mallory Hyde. Every person was a delight to work with on this project.

Thanks to Ashley LeBlanc, who provided a fresh perspective on several of the chapters; Frank Lunn, who, in 2002 at a writer's conference in Los Angeles, exposed me to Someday Isle; David Cook, my longtime friend who taught me to see, feel, and trust. He authored one of my favorite books and movies of all time: *Seven Days in Utopia: Golf's Sacred Journey.*

Special thanks to my wife, Madeline, who endured reading aloud with me at least six different versions of this book.

Without a doubt, I am one of the most fortunate people in the world. I thank God every day for allowing me the opportunity to live my dream.

To each person who reads this book, I hope that it will inspire you to your greatest success.

A Collection of Quotations

from
*Quit Drifting, Lift the Fog,
and Get Lucky*

"At one time or another, everyone has to identify and address the shocking gap between what they expected from their career or life and the reality of what they are experiencing."

"There is no grand conspiracy preventing you from achieving what you want in life."

"Your success and happiness will ultimately be molded by your decisions, not by temporary conditions happening around you."

"Without integrity, nothing else really matters. It doesn't matter what you say if no one trusts you. And it doesn't matter how committed, skilled, courageous, or optimistic you are if people don't believe you'll honor your words."

"The challenges you face are not there to destroy you; they are there to redirect you to the path that's right for you."

"You may not have control over everything that has happened to you, but you control your next move."

"To achieve happiness and success—however you define it—you first have to feel great about yourself."

"Most of the time, people don't quit because their challenge is unreasonable or unrealistic. They give up because they get impatient. . . they flee right before they would have found success."

"Be careful of shortcuts. Believe it or not, most of the time the shortcuts become much longer routes."

"Most people fall into two distinct categories—doers or drifters. The doers . . . are on a mission to achieve their goals. The drifters allow external circumstances to determine their next move."

"You can tell a lot about the direction a person's life is

heading by watching the people with whom they choose to spend time."

"Your job should be fulfilling, not a burden. It is a gift and privilege."

"Long-term success and happiness require you to live within consistent operating rules that do not change based on the situation of the day."

"In reality, the bad is not as bad as it seems, but neither is the good as good as you think."

"Everyone is just one blood test, stress test, X-ray, or serious accident away from a life-changing moment. There's no good reason to put off becoming the person you want to be."

"It is difficult to become a positive, committed, lucky person if you continually surround yourself with negative, lukewarm, whining people."

"Complacency is the root of mediocrity—success's worst enemy—even more destructive than failure."

"The paradox of change is the best time to do it is when it may seem to be the least necessary."

"The greatest desire of everyone—whether friends, family, employees, or clients—is to be appreciated."

"People forgive and forget judgment errors, but rarely does anyone forget integrity mistakes."

"You may want people to allow you the grace of not counting minor commitments. But people will judge you on what *they* think about you, not what *you believe* they should think about you."

"Truth is absolute, not relative. You need to be honest with 100-percent precision as best you can."

"It is not fair for you to transfer your emergency to become someone else's emergency."

"Two great fog generators . . . are constant worry and persistent negative emotions. Both . . . create fog so thick that you can't see how to move forward."

"Worrying doesn't prevent anything from happening. . . . Worry will paralyze you—and not much good happens when you're paralyzed by worry."

"When you don't know the true facts, the tendency is to imagine the worst—things you fear will happen—and then make assumptions based on your imagination. Those assumptions are almost always wrong. Quit imagining and reacting to what you don't know."

"Optimistic people see opportunity. Negative people can't see through their own fog to the potential right in front of them."

"You get what you give. If you want to be around people who are positive, optimistic, and eager to live life, your attitude has to be the same."

"Give your family your best, not just your leftovers from work."

"Regardless of what is going on, something can be done, and the next move is mine."

"It's okay to fail—everyone fails at one time or another—but it's not okay to keep failing at the same thing. And it's not okay to ignore the lessons from your failures."

"Some people want the truth to be different so badly, they shun reality. They either trample the truth or ignore it."

"It's never a good idea to lie to yourself, no matter how painful the truth may be. You have to respect the truth."

"I developed strength from failure. The scars from my failures eventually healed and became beauty marks ... When I look back, I see failure taught me humility, perseverance, and courage. I learned that my failures were important lessons that helped lead me toward my happiness and success."

"One of my most difficult, but most important, lessons was to learn to forgive myself for my own gaffes. I had to find peace within myself."

"Forgiveness had to be a gift, not a trade exchanged with an expectation of something in return. If I expected something in return, I was not forgiving at all; I was trading."

"To be successful, you don't need to know everything. You just need to ask the right questions and fill in the gaps of what you are missing as quickly as you can."

"Your past doesn't have a future, but you do. Keep learning, improving, and moving forward. The direction of your next step will reveal itself along the way."

"You can't just want, hope, or wish for luck to show up. You must actively throw yourself in luck's path."

"The more you learn, the luckier you will be."

"A common trait among successful people is that they are avid readers."

"Positive people attract luck like a magnet."

"Ignoring a conflict does not cause it to go away. In fact, it nourishes it and allows it to fester and become worse. It will gnaw at and irritate you. That isn't good for anyone."

"*Someday I will,*' or '*Someday I'm going to*' are the rallying cries of the residents of Someday Isle. Never in history has a situation improved on its own while people sat basking in the sun, doing nothing on Someday Isle."

"There is no such thing as the perfect time. You will not get much of anything done unless you go ahead and do something before the timing is completely perfect."

"If you multitask while doing multiple important things at once, you will wind up doing multiple important things badly at the same time."

"One of the beautiful things about mentoring—the coach learns as much as, or even more than, the person who was being coached."

"Don't be so busy making a living that you forget how to live."

About the Author

David Cottrell is president and CEO of Corner-Stone Leadership. He worked with many of today's greatest organizations, mentoring leaders to peak performance.

Before founding CornerStone, David held leadership positions with Xerox and FedEx and led the successful turnaround of a Chapter 11 company. He has shared his personal development and leadership lessons in person with more than four hundred thousand people worldwide.

David has authored more than twenty-five books, including the perennial bestselling *Monday Morning Leadership* and his autobiography, *Grace Upon Grace*. His books are available in more than a dozen languages and have sold over two million copies worldwide.

The Next Step—Implement Quit Drifting, Lift the Fog, and Get Lucky *into Your Organization*

QUIT DRIFTING, LIFT THE FOG, AND GET LUCKY POWERPOINT PRESENTATION

This cost-effective, downloadable PowerPoint includes a professionally prepared PowerPoint deck. $99.95

Visit www.CornerStoneLeadership.com

KEYNOTE PRESENTATION

Invite author David Cottrell to inspire your team and help create greater success for your organization. Each presentation is designed to set a solid foundation for both organizational and personal achievement.

Contact Michele@DavidCottrell.com

FREE! *Quit Drifting, Lift the Fog, and Get Lucky* Reproducible Handouts

You can lead your discussion group at work, home, school, or church through ***Quit Drifting, Lift the Fog, and Get Lucky*** with our free, five-session, small group guide and reproducible handouts.

You do not have to be an expert in facilitation to lead your group. The FREE small group guide provides everything you need.

Download at www.CornerStoneLeadership.com

FREE! Time Management Assessment and Goal Setting Process Worksheet

Download at www.CornerStoneLeadership.com

The
Quit Drifting, Lift the Fog and Get Lucky
Book Package

Includes all 7 books pictured for

only $79.95!

(A $112 value!)

For additional leadership resources,
visit www.CornerStoneLeadership.com